Domaining Guide

How to Profit from Domain Names

By Jerome Robertson

CONTENTS

CHAPTER 1 - INTRODUCTION
Prepare for Liftoff!
Who is Jerome Robertson?

CHAPTER 2 – ACTION PLAN
How to Get Started
Steps to Take

CHAPTER 3 - GETTING STARTED: DREAMING OF DOLLAR SIGNS
What is a Domain Name?
Virtual Real Estate (Without the Slump)
The Boom is Yet to Come
How to Register a Domain
Five Ways to Save Money When Registering Domains

CHAPTER 4 - DOMAIN EXTENSIONS
Types of Top Level Domains
.COM – The Obvious Choice
.NET – Second Best?
Dot-Others – Opportunity Knocks
nGTLDs – Trendy Speculation
ccTLDs – Home Sweet Home
.AU – Australia
.CA – Canada
.CN – China
.DE – Germany
.ES – Spain
.FR – France
.NL – Netherlands

.IN – India
.SE – Sweden
.UK – United Kingdom
.US – United States
Other ccTLDs
Top ccTLD Sales
International Domain Names (IDNs)
Conclusion: Buy for the End User

CHAPTER 5 - DOMAINING NICHES
Specializing Spells Opportunity

CHAPTER 6 - HOW TO VALUE DOMAINS
The Importance of Understanding Value
Wholesale and Retail Value
Keeping Track of Reported Sales
Popularity Matters
Traffic is King
Getting Down to Business
Developed Domains
Short, Brandable Names
Commercial Appraisals Don't Matter
Free Appraisals
Ahead of the Trend
Conclusion

CHAPTER 7 - BUYING DOMAINS
The Buyer's Advantage
Quality vs. Quantity
Where to Buy Domains
Buying Expired & Pre-Released Domains
The Domain Deletion Cycle
The Backorder Process
Why Buy Expired Domains?
Registration Fee Punts

CHAPTER 8 - TRANSFERRING DOMAINS
Change of Account or Registrant Transfer
Domain Transfer or Registrar Transfer
Ensuring a Secure Transaction

CHAPTER 9 - SELLING DOMAINS
Why Sell?
Passive & Proactive Selling
Selling to Other Domainers
Selling to End Users
What Not to Use

CHAPTER 10 - NEGOTIATION
Five Negotiating Strategies for Buying a Domain Name
Five Negotiating Strategies for Selling a Domain Name

CHAPTER 11 - MAKING MONEY THROUGH DOMAIN PARKING
Domain Parking – The Basics
How to Park Your Domains
Step 1: Select a Parking Company
Step 2: Register
Step 3: Select Keywords and a Template
Step 4: Set the Domain Nameserver to the Parking Company
Step 5: Performance Testing

CHAPTER 12 - DOMAIN DEVELOPMENT
Taking the Car Out of the Garage
What Domains Should You Develop?
Step-By-Step Development
Monetizing a Developed Site

CHAPTER 13 - DOMAIN LAW
Trademark Issues
Anti-Cybersquatting Consumer Protection Act (ACPA)
UDRP and the Three-Pronged Test

WIPO Arbitration and Mediation Center
Cyber Bullying
Reverse Domain Name Hijacking
Front Running (Domain Sniffing)
Domain Security and Theft
Setting up a Company to Run Your Domain Business
Tax Treatment of Domains
Five Summarizing Tips for Domainers

CHAPTER 14 - GENERAL ECONOMIC TRENDS
Domain Growth
The Future of Business

CHAPTER 15 - CONCLUSION
Ready, Set, GO!
The Next Step...

CHAPTER 16 - FURTHER READING
Leading Blogs:
Domain Forums:

MORE INFORMATION

In addition to authoring *Domaining Guide*, Jerome Robertson runs the website **DomainingGuide.com**. You can learn more about Jerome, and obtain free supplemental materials, at DomainingGuide.com.

Chapter 1 - Introduction

In This Chapter...

> ✓ **Prepare for Liftoff!**

Prepare for Liftoff!

Thanks for purchasing this eBook! Much like you, I'm extremely excited about the domain industry and the opportunities available, now and in the future.

Domaining presents a very unique investment alternative since you are able to create your own rules. You don't need to take out a mortgage or drop a major down payment to secure your future wealth. In fact, you can easily create a passive income stream for only a modest amount of money.

Domaining can be whatever you want it to be. It can be a hobby or it can be career. You can get started by spending only a couple hours each week or you can totally immerse yourself in the industry. Honestly, it's all up to you. The more time and effort you put into it, the more money you'll be able to make.

The important part is that you take advantage of the industry's unique opportunities and advantages. Read this book, meditate on the ideas, take notes on the key concepts, formulate your own strategy for success, and <u>act</u> on it. Many people struggle to make their dreams a reality, but it all boils down to action. You can read everything there is to know about domaining, but until you implement your knowledge nothing will get done. But I don't expect that to be a problem for you; the simple fact that you purchased this eBook shows you're a person of action!

My objective in this book is to paint a complete picture of the domain industry and the key strategies for success that I have learned in my over 10 years of domaining. I will show you how to sift, sort, and select the domains that are made of gold so you can strike it rich by using proven techniques. Nothing will work 100% of the time, but this book will give you everything you need to build a strong portfolio and become consistently profitable.

But let me warn you about one thing – this is not intended to be a get-rich quick scheme of any kind. If that's what you're looking for then you should look somewhere else; I don't deal with that kind of stuff. Instead, I'll show you how to make money with domain names by taking calculated risks and making wise business decisions.

With that said, it's time to buckle up and prepare for lift off! I'm excited to have you along for the ride.

Who is Jerome Robertson?

This is a practical book about domaining. Will it help you? Is it accurate? Who am I to author it?

I have been a domainer since 2006. I learnt domaining the hard way, by making lots of mistakes, and learning from them. It's probably the way most people learn domaining, but it is certainly not the best say.

In the last couple of years, I've had a substantial number of people approach me and ask for my advice about getting into domaining. They have many questions. They may have already bought some domains, and not know how to sell them. Figuring it all out on your own isn't easy, and is bound to result in a lot of costly errors and time wasted.

If you are in that situation, then you are not alone. While there are a lot of answers already out there on the Internet, this book provides a complete guide to getting started in the industry. You can spend hundreds of hours digging through old forum threads and blog posts trying to piece together the information you need to succeed, or you can learn the information you need in a simple and straightforward fashion.

I try to cover everything that you need in this book, but if there is anything I've missed, or any further questions you have, I'm happy to help. You can simply contact me through my website DomainingGuide.com.

Jerome Robertson

Chapter 2 – Action Plan

In This Chapter...

- ✓ **How to Get Started**
- ✓ **Steps To Take**
- ✓ **Domaining Myths Busted**

How to Get Started

I know that you're a person of action; otherwise you wouldn't have bought this book. So, you're eager to get going and want to buy your first domain name.

However, and this is important, you should not start buying domains until you've read all or most of this book. Even then, it is still a good idea not to buy right away. You will want to spend some time watching the market and checking that what you think is correct really is correct.

If you were about to invest in real estate, you wouldn't simply buy the first house you saw that looked cool. Instead, you'd focus on a particular neighborhood, see what houses are for sale in the neighborhood, and what prices they sell at and why, who the different real estate agents are; what features of a home make it sell for more, and so on.

The same applies to domains. There is just as much to learn about domains before you invest in them as there is about real estate. While most domainers end up losing money when starting off, there is no reason needlessly waste your hard-earned money. If it really were easy to make lots of money domaining, most people would be doing it already.

Steps to Take

The order that this book is set out in is the order of the action plan for you to take. Chapter 2 provides background information on domains. Then…

Step 1 - Choose which **domain extension(s)** you want to invest in. This is like choosing which neighborhood in town you want to buy real estate in. Chapter 4 covers the basics of domain extensions. For most beginners, the best choice is .com or possibly, depending on where you live, your local country code domain.

Step 2 – Choose a particular **niche** you want to invest in. Just as you can't start out by investing in houses, condos, strip malls, and industrial properties, you can't just invest in domains if you want to do it profitably. You need to find a particular niche you are interested in, can concentrate on, and do well in. Chapter 5 covers the basics of choosing a niche.

Step 3 – Learn how to **value a domain**. You now know what domains you are interested in, but what price should you buy them at, and what price should you sell them at? To determine this, you need to learn about domain valuation, and that is what Chapter 6 teaches you.

Step 4 – You're finally ready to **buy a domain**! But how? And where? You'll learn this in Chapter 7.

Step 5 - You've bought a domain – how do you **transfer it?** That's what Chapter 8 covers.

Step 6 – So now you've got all these great domains, and you've bought them all at great prices, but obviously, you haven't made any money yet. To make money, you need to **sell your domains**. Chapter 9 will help you do that.

Step 7 – You're on your way – now you're buying and selling domains. But you can do even better yet buy learning how **negotiation** for buying a selling domains. Chapter 10 will start you on your way to being a better negotiator.

You could technically stop there, and just rinse and repeat. The rest of the chapters of the book are more advanced topics. Chapters 11 and 12 will help you make more money on domains you own through parking and development. Chapter 13 will help you avoid legal fees by teaching you the basics of domain law, and running a domain business. Chapter 14 deals with the economics of the domain industry. Chapter 15 wraps everything up and the Chapter 16 lets you know how to advance further once you've completed this book.

Chapter 3 - Getting Started: Dreaming of Dollar Signs

In This Chapter...

> ✓ What is a Domain Name?
> ✓ Virtual Real Estate (Without the Slump)
> ✓ The Boom is Yet to Come
> ✓ How to Register a Domain
> ✓ Five Ways to Save Money When Registering

What is a Domain Name?

Imagine if people were known by their telephone numbers instead of their names. Not only would it be difficult to memorize a long string of numbers for every person you knew, but every time a friend decided to move and get a new phone number, you'd have to start calling them by their newly listed name. It would get confusing after a while, right?

Of course!

This is the story of how domain names came into existence.

Most computers that are connected to the internet are defined by a unique number, known as an IP address (ex. 123.456.78.910).

When the internet first began, websites were found by typing in these lengthy strands of numbers and accessing the host computers. Since these IP addresses were hard to remember and subject to change, there was an apparent need for a better system.

Just as we would give descriptive names to our friends (in the same way that family names were originally developed), domain names are easy-to-remember descriptions for the websites they represent.

There are a number of ways domain names can be used to describe the content, such as (but not limited to):

- Location: www.NewYork.com
- Abbreviation: www.USA.com
- Description: www.BigCity.com
- Person's Name: www.MichaelJordan.com
- Product: www.Vodka.com
- Services/Job Title: www.Lawyers.com
- Combinations: www.NewYorkLawyers.com
- Add-Ons: www.FreeMusic.com

The options are limitless!

The easier a domain name is to remember (while connecting with its content, product, or services), the more valuable it will be.

Virtual Real Estate (Without the Slump)

Domains names are often considered the Internet's equivalent to real estate; they are online properties that can be bought, sold, developed, parked, and rented – but most of all, much like real estate, they consistently grow in value year after year due to limited supply and growing demand.

So why should you invest in domains instead of more traditional alternatives such as real estate, stocks, bonds, and mutual funds? Simple...you want to make more money.

The whole purpose of investing is to make money, right?

Sure enough, the domain name industry is among the fastest growing investment opportunities in the world and has seen tremendous growth in the past few years.

Domains are being snapped up at incredible rates with around 100,000 new names being purchased *every day*!

Much like prime-real estate in a packed city – there is a growing demand for great domain names, but a very limited supply...a guaranteed formula for growth.

What started out as a hobby for techies ten years ago has turned into a business opportunity that is ready to explode! According to USA Today, the industry's market value could be over $4 billion.

> **Domain Data – What's In a Domain?**
>
> Domain names can contain letters (a-z), numbers (0-9), and the hyphen character – although they cannot begin or end with a hyphen.
>
> The maximum allowable length for a domain name is 67 characters with the suffix included (ex. ".com" would count as four characters).

The Boom is Yet to Come

You've probably heard some of the stories and thought to yourself that "it's too late to get in." You know what I'm talking about...

- Men.com selling for $1.32 million
- DataRecovery.com selling for $1.75 million
- CreditCards.com selling for $2.5 million
- CreditCheck.com selling for $3 million
- Discover.com selling for $5 million
- Business.com selling for $7.5 million
- Porn.com selling for $9.5 million
- Fund.com selling for $10 million
- Sex.com selling for an estimated $12-14 million

Are you going to have a sale like that any time soon? Probably not...but don't worry, what we've seen happen so far is only the tip of the iceberg.

Look over the short list of domains above and imagine how many others could be comparable in value. I would estimate there are hundreds of similarly valued domains that could fetch seven-figures in today's marketplace... and thousands of other domains that could easily sell for six-figures.

No, that doesn't mean you can find a $10 gem tomorrow that will make you a millionaire, but you *can* earn huge profits if you treat domaining as a long-term investment and business.

Put your seatbelt on and get ready to learn... because I'm going to give you everything you need to know to make money in the domain industry today while also preparing you for long-term success.

How to Register a Domain

To register a domain name, you'll need to set up an account with an ICANN approved domain name registrar or reseller.

A registrar acts as a middleman for you; taking your information (and money) so they can register the domain name on your behalf. For a full list of accredited registrars, visit InterNIC.

> **Not on the List?**
> If a registrar is not on the list, it is possible that they are a reseller for a larger registrar – such as Namecheap for Enom.

Some are less expensive than others while providing the same basic service. Although you're often told that "you get what you pay for," this is not necessarily the case with domain registrars.

Sure, some won't try to up-sell you as much as others, but they'll charge you more money for hassle-free service. Personally, I don't mind a few advertisements here and there and have never noticed a difference in service between a $10 registrar and a $25 one.

If you don't want to go through the entire list of registrars to find one that works for you, then take a look at some of my favorites:

GoDaddy.com – By far the most popular registrar on the net, Go Daddy sells two times more domain names than its closest competitor. Go Daddy has everything you need with plenty of options no matter what you're looking for.
    Pros: Excellent pricing, and tons of coupons. If you have enough domains to get assigned an account manager, service is good.
    Cons: Aggressive promotions and cluttered interface. Service is quick but often poorly informed unless you have an account manager.

Namecheap.com – Although the domain name doesn't make you think "quality," Namecheap delivers a solid service with an impressive control panel.
    Pros: Free email, URL forwarding, free transfers, and cheap pricing. Intuitive system and good support.

Uniregistry.com – The registrar of choice for large domain portfolio holders.

Pros: Intuitive interface and decent pricing.

Cons: Service can be poor unless you are a big shot.

Other Recommendations: Dynadot.com, NameSilo.com, Netistrar.com, and Fabulous.com.

Getting an account with a domain registrar is easy and shouldn't take longer than five minutes.

You'll need to fill out the standard forms with your name, address, phone number, and email address. Make sure you provide accurate information because registrars can take away your domains if they have reason to believe you've provided false information.

Once you have your account, you can start searching for your domain of choice.

> **Warning:** If you want to register a domain with a registrar that hasn't been highly recommended by a trusted source, make sure you check it out beforehand! You should know what you're looking for in a registrar and find one that suits your specific needs. If you want to check on their reputation, go to the NamePros message board to read about other people's experiences.

Five Ways to Save Money When Registering Domains

Even though domain registration is already quite inexpensive, there are still ways that you can save significant amounts of money if you're registering tens, hundreds, or thousands of domains each year.

Check out how fast a savings of $2 per domain could add up...

- $20 after 10 domains
- $100 after 50 domains
- $200 after 100 domains
- $1000 after 500 domains
- And so on...

And what's better, you'll see savings like this year after year – every time you register or renew a domain. Here are five ways to save money when registering your domain names:

1. **Shop Around** – You've seen the list of registrars and you've seen my recommendations; check them out. Don't feel like you need to have all your domains at one place, because if you do you'll miss out on special offers elsewhere.
2. **Use Coupons** – Whenever you purchase a domain name, search Google for any coupons that might be available.
3. **Premium Memberships** – If you're going to be a big-time buyer, then you might want to purchase an annual premium membership at your favorite registrar. One warning though – do the math to make sure you'll actually save money in the long run.

4. **Shop Smart** – Don't buy every domain name that catches your eye. Instead, try to stick to the cream of the crop – the names that *really* stick out. These will be the most valuable – and you'll avoid holding on to domains that you never use or sell before they expire.
5. **Transferring** – If you're paying too much for renewals each year (which you shouldn't have to do with coupons or premium memberships), then you should consider paying to transfer your domains instead of renewing them. Transfers often cost less and come with a one-year extended registration for free.

Chapter 4 - Domain Extensions

In This Chapter...

- ✓ Types of Top Level Domains
- ✓ .COM – The Obvious Choice
- ✓ .NET – Second Best?
- ✓ Dot Others – Opportunity Knocks
- ✓ The new gTLDs – Trendy Speculation?
- ✓ ccTLDs – Home Sweet Home
- ✓ Tracking the Trends
- ✓ Conclusion: Buy for the End User

Types of Top Level Domains

A top level domain (TLD) is the last part of a domain name, which always follows the final dot. The Internet Assigned Numbers Authority (IANA) currently divides the top level domains into three groups:

1. **Country Code Top Level Domain** (ccTLD): Used by a country or dependent territory.

2. **Generic Top Level Domain** (gTLD): Used by organizations, although some of the most popular gTLDs are unrestricted.
3. **Infrastructure Top Level Domain** (iTLD): Only two have ever been used: .arpa and .root.

When it comes to domaining, you can quickly forget about iTLDs. Done? Okay, good...

...but ccTLDs and gTLDs are different with some of them being extremely valuable, .com in particular.

While there are many ccTLDs and gTLDs out there, you don't need to purchase them all to make money. In fact, you **shouldn't** purchase them all! Too often inexperienced investors get caught up in trendy TLDs before analyzing the value and ensuring their investment is worthwhile.

In this chapter, I'm going to discuss the TLDs that matter. You'll find out which TLDs are worth investing in, the ones you should hold off on, and the others that you should avoid at all costs.

Why am I starting the book by reviewing domain extensions?
Think of domain extensions as the part of town that you are located in. Real estate in some parts of town will be profitable; and in other parts of town will not. Investing in the right domain extensions will make the difference between being a big success and losing lots of money. Many who invested in .com domains are doing well; almost everyone who invested in .mobi domains lost money. While profits can, and are, made in almost every domain extension, some extensions are much easier to make money from.

> **Top Level Domains – Too Many To List Here**
> For a full list of TLDs that are out there, check out the official list at IANA.org. Don't be scared off by the long list, I'll quickly narrow it down for you so that you can focus on the few that are worth your time.

.COM – The Obvious Choice

The .com domain was one of the original TLDs established in January 1985 and has grown into the most recognizable TLD on the internet. .Com domain names are usually considered to be at least ten times more valuable than any matching name with a different extension.

Although .com domains were originally intended for commercial entities, the TLD gained popularity when it became unrestricted in the mid 1990's. This allowed anybody with a computer to register their own .com domain – and many people did.

Thanks to the internet's tremendous growth around this time, the .com quickly turned into the most popular TLD on the internet and has remained that way ever since – even with many other TLDs becoming unrestricted.

.Com domains are particularly valuable for companies with an American or international audience, which ultimately means they have the most value of any domain extension worldwide.

Positives
-Unmatched popularity.
-Great for branding.
-Always growing in value.

Negatives
-None

Did You Know?
As I'm writing this... 9 of the top 10 most popular sites on the web are .com sites (according to Alexa), with the only exception being Wikipedia.org.

.NET – Second Best?

This domain extension is .com's little brother; it does the same thing, just not as well. This TLD was also one of the originals released in 1985 and, much like the .com, it also became unrestricted within a few years.

For quite some time, small businesses and domainers have had to "settle" for the .net extension when the .com was already taken.

While the .net does have value, it is greatly diminished because it loses so much traffic and branding power to the .com with the same name. In fact, many successful .net companies have ended up purchasing the .com TLD after some time because of this problem.

Aside from being much less valuable than the .com, the .net is a difficult TLD to brand. Why? Because most people will still type in ".com".

Positives
-Recognizable
-Good sales history
-Better than most gTLDs

Negatives
-Will lose traffic to .com
-More difficult to brand than .com or ccTLDs.

Dot-Others – Opportunity Knocks

There are tons of TLDs out there that you can make money with. In fact, there are many domain names that provide extremely high return on investment in every TLD out there. The fact is, if you have a great name there will be a market for it. Here are a few of the other TLDs that you should know about:

.ORG – Non-Profit for Big Profit
This domain extension has been popularized by the non-profit companies that have set up shop. Some of the most recognizable websites on the internet have used .org including Wikipedia.org (ranked 9th overall), Mininova.org (ranked 53rd), and Craigslist.org (ranked 66th).

While there is certainly money to be had with .org domain extensions, it is certainly behind .com and .net in most cases.

.BIZ – Will it Ever Mature?
.Biz is a domain extension intended for businesses. Since it's a generic extension, it will always compete with the .com, .net, .info, and ccTLDs. Although it won't ever come close to the major ccTLDs or gTLDs, there is room for a decent return on investment if you play your cards right. However, as always, be careful to not be too speculative.

.ASIA – Landrush Over
I've never really understood this one. First of all, it's an English domain extension for a non-English region. Secondly, they already have ccTLDs that are quite popular and doing just fine. While I'm sure there will be some money made in buying and flipping, I don't see a whole lot of end users for this extension, which ultimately means that I don't see a lot of potential. It's a huge market though, so only time will tell.

.INFO – Four Letters Too Much?
In 2000, ICANN agreed to release seven new gTLDs - .biz, .info, .name, .pro, .aero, .coop, and .museum. Of the group, .info has been the most successful by a long shot.

There have been over 4 million domains registered with almost 2 million being used. This domain extension is bound to be a popular item for a long time, although it has a very limited ceiling price since it will usually be used for information websites, which can't be easily monetized.

nGTLDs – Trendy Speculation

Plenty of new GTLDs have been released since 2013, and there are still more to come. Most of them will be risky investments – some will pay off and many others won't. However, if you track the market closely, know how to gauge value, and understand ways to maximize your profits then you may well make money (the market is really too immature at this point to be sure).

The purpose behind all these new GTLDs is to ~~make ICANN lots of money~~ give consumers a greater choice of extensions. The thought was that pretty much every term you may want to register in the older gtlds was already registered – you can instead register the term in a new gtld.

There are several types of new gtlds. The first are generic ones – such as .xyz, .club, and .web. These are meant to compete head on with older gtlds such as .net or .biz.

Then there are geographic gtlds, such as .london and .tokyo. These are meant more to compete with country domains, which we will discuss in a moment.

There are also many specialized gtlds, such as .blog, .legal, and .archi that are intended to focus on a niche audience.

One important thing to note about the nGTLDs is pricing. Typically, domains have traditionally cost about $10 to $20 to register.

However, the registries can price the nGTLDs however they wish. For premium domains (and often domains that are only moderately good), the registries are pricing the domains at hundreds or even thousands of dollars per year. This makes it difficult for domainers to make a profit on – imagine holding 100 domains that cost $1,000 per year to renew. The high renewal prices tend to squeeze domainers out of the market.

Follow the Money

The good part with new gtlds is that there has been a fair bit demand and buzz within the domaining community. People have been paying top dollar for great names such as (but hardly limited to):

- 1.xyz for $182,971
- 88.xin for $180,000
- 9.xyz for $175,166
- tube.webcam for $175,000
- sex.live for $160,000
- wine.club for $140,000

Nonetheless, the major concern is that the market is being flooded by a plethora of alternative domain names. Why would someone buy a domain in your extension when they have 2,000 other extensions to choose from?

As for investing in the nGTLDs, the best route is: (a) buy top keywords in the best promoted ngtlds; and (b) buy terms that make sense as a left of the dot / right of the dot combination. So, a term like hotels will likely have at least some value in any nGTLD. A domain like stock.photo is a left of the dot / right of the dot combination that just makes a lot of sense, and in fact, is even shorter than stockphoto.com.

Conclusion

No one can say for sure what the future of nGTLDs is. Anyone who tells you otherwise is lying.

My belief is that the new extensions will most likely impact .info, .asia, .mobi, .pro, .biz, and other domains that have yet to find a place in mainstream domaining, but they will have no chance of significantly damaging more established extensions.

We can safely say that nGTLDs are a highly speculative investment. While calculated risks should be taken, and it may well be worth your while to invest in some of the highest quality nGTLDs, nGTLDs shouldn't play a major role in any domainer's portfolio.

Positives
-Could work if it was every adopted by the marketplace.
-Supported by domainers

Negatives
-Highly speculative
-Lack of end-users
-High renewal fees

ccTLDs – Home Sweet Home

Country code domains have become extremely valuable to end users, since they are aimed directly at their target markets.

While domainers play a large role in the rise and fall of domain sales, the end user sets the ultimate value. If a domain can make somebody a lot of money, then that's what it is worth.

While .com and .net domains have an unlimited target market, which increases their value, there is still a lot to be said for ccTLDs.

ccTLDs are able to do something that generic domains cannot, they can shrink the marketplace and increase the visitor value by branding themselves for a specific audience.

Here are a few examples of ccTLDs being more valuable to companies than a gTLD:
- SEO.de (SEO is a universal term for "Search Engine Optimization") was purchased for $70,000. This domain name distinguishes itself as being distinctly German, making it more effective in a German marketplace than SEO.com (which would be assumed to be English).
- DJMusic.ca is more appropriate for a small Canadian DJ franchise than DJMusic.com. The latter would be more expensive while also overextending their boundaries. It is also a more effective domain name than CanadianDJMusic.com, which was most likely another option for this business.
- Recycle.co.uk was purchased for over $300,000 USD. The company has set the site up as a UK Recycling program.

Because of its specific use, this domain name brands the website better than Recycle.com or UKRecycle.com.

ccTLDs provide a key advantage for regionally based businesses, because visitors know they are dealing with a local entity – which is not the case with generic TLDs. One issue, however, is that a ccTLD will always lose a portion of its traffic to its .com counterpart.

> **Definition: "End User"**
> By "end user," I am referring to the company or individual that will ultimately purchase the domain for the purpose of developing it. Basically – anybody other than a domainer.

In the next few pages I'm going to be covering some of the most popular ccTLDs available.

.AU – Australia
Population = 28,925,291

.AU domain names can only be registered by individuals, companies, and organizations that are located in Australia. Because of this, the domain hasn't attracted many (if any) foreign attention, but within Australia it's a different story.

At one point in 2004 the .au TLD was actually more popular within Australia's borders than any other extension including .com.

While this domain is one of the more interesting ccTLDs, it's a risky one for domainers because of the limited aftermarket, and the fact that there is a good chance that Australia will be moving from .com.au to .au. That being said, if you live in Australia, and stick with top tier domains, you can do will in .au.

.CA – Canada

Population = 36,332,944

One of the fastest growing ccTLDs in the past few years, .ca is starting to get major recognition in the domaining world – even though many aren't eligible to register a .ca domain.

While .ca domains can only be registered by entities connected with Canada, they have been marketed so well within this region that it is often considered an advantage to have a .ca domain for any website with a Canadian-only audience (yes, often better than .com).

With domain sales growing larger each month, this ccTLD is worth investigating.

.CN – China

Population = 1,383,164,315

When you have over 1 billion people living in a single country, you can expect the ccTLD to catch people's attention... especially when foreign registration is permitted.

.CN is used by many sites that market to mainland China, although there have been some concerns over domain hoarding by foreigners investing on speculated growth. This creates a Catch-22 scenario: foreign domainers need sites to be developed and used by the Chinese population for the ccTLD to grow, but the Chinese population cannot develop and use sites when many of the domain names are owned by foreigners (nor will they pay a premium for an unproven extension).

.DE – Germany
Population = 82,210,000

This is the most popular ccTLD and second only to .com in the number of registrations for any extension available worldwide.

Although you must have an administrative contact in Germany to register a domain name, there has been a lot of foreign investment by companies marketing to Germany, domainers taking advantage of a strong extension, and others looking to play on the .de extension (which mean "of" in Spanish, French, Romanian, and Portuguese).

.DE is much more popular in Germany than any other extension.

.ES – Spain
Population = 46,056,862

It was very difficult and costly to register a .es domain before November 2005, when there were a number of restrictions and limitations put on the extension. However, .es domains can now be registered by anybody and they've been growing in popularity ever since.

Because of the demographics, it is common for Spanish, English, and Catalan words to be used in the domain name, although Spanish is the most popular.

The domain is growing in popularity in Spain. Domainers can expect .es domains to continue gaining value as the home market becomes more accepting of its presence.

.FR – France
Population = 64,705,235

While this extension has seen limited growth in recent years, it has also shown promise through a number of solid sales over the past two years.

.FR is very popular in France, but hasn't reached full speed in the domaining community because of the registration restrictions which include a presence in France and a local administrative contact.

If these restrictions are ever lifted, you can expect much more activity in the domaining world.

.NL – Netherlands
Population = 16,987,179

.NL was the first ccTLD to ever be registered and, despite the limited population in the region, it remains one of the most popular ccTLDs around.

The extension is extremely popular in the Netherlands and almost 70% of the registered domains are used by businesses, with over 62% of registered domain names actively used.

Dutch is the most commonly used language for .nl domains, closely followed by English.

.IN – India
Population = 1,328,953,585

Before this extension's restrictions were lifted in 2005, only 7000 .in domain names had been registered. Now there are over 2,000,000 – and still many more great names available.

If you're looking to invest with a limited budget, then .in is one of the best options for you. With 1.3 billion people in the country, this ccTLD has nowhere to go but up. More and more people from India are getting the internet, so traffic is bound to continue growing over time to provide more potential for monetizing websites. For more information about this ccTLD, visit INForum.

.SE – Sweden
Population = 9,861,722

Up until April 2003, registration for .se domains was very restrictive – but since it has lightened the domain name has grown in popularity.

The domain has surprised many with high-end sales within such a small region, but the extension is the most popular in Sweden and has a lot of commercial and end user potential.

Domaining isn't about how much the top domain names sell for, but rather the return on investment. Even though Sweden is a rather small region, you can expect this ccTLD to grow in value for a long time.

.UK – United Kingdom

Population = 65,164,978

.UK is the fifth largest TLD and third rated ccTLD with over 10 million registered domains.

To make matters more interesting, traditionally you were required to use a second-level domain name such as .co.uk for registration. However, .uk has since been released, with all existing .co.uk receiving a right of registration of the .uk for 5 years.

This extension is very popular in the United Kingdom and is expected to continue gaining value in the future since it has been so well received in the UK and throughout the internet.

.US – United States
Population = 324,438,366

This extension has struggled to get accepted in the United States, as it is much less popular than .com, .net, and .org – but many domainers continue to hope for growth in the future.

Regardless of its current popularity, there have been several large .us domain sales in the past few years. One concern, however, is whether the extension is being used regularly by end users or simply bought and sold within the domaining community.

Other ccTLDs

While there are over 200 ccTLDs out there, some are worth checking out more than others. Here are a few others that are worth investigating: .ar (Argentina), .br (Brazil), .ch (Switzerland), eu (European Union), .it (Italy), and .ru (Russia).

In addition to this, some ccTLDs have been repurposed into generic TLDs. That is, although they have been assigned to a particular country, the country's registry has marketed them as being for general use. The best known examples of this are:

.tv (Tuvalu) – marketed as "television" for video websites
.co (Columbia) – marketed as "company" and as short for ".com"
.me (Montenegro) – marketed as a hack and as a generic
.io (British Indian Ocean Territory) – popular as a generic among startups

These sorts of repurposed ccTLDs market to an international audience, and therefore can have the potential of higher demand, and therefore higher value.

Top ccTLD Sales

One way to gauge what the best ccTLDs to invest in is to look at which ccTLDs have the highest sales. Courtesy of Ron Jackson at DNJournal, we can see that the find a list of the top 100 cctlds in the year to date. Going through that list as of the date of writing, the list includes:

.uk – 14 sales
.de – 13 sales
.co – 8 sales
.nl – 7 sales
.tv – 7 sales
.io – 6 sales
.ca – 4 sales
.au – 2 sales
.in – 1 sales

This gives you some idea about the relative popularity of each extension, and the ease or difficulty with which you'll be able to sell a domain in a particular ccTLD.

International Domain Names (IDNs)

IDN stands for "International Domain Name." The normal domains that you are used to using are all written with the standard ASCII characters with which we are familiar - the letters A to Z, the numbers 0 to 9, and the hyphen. That works well for English, but the fact is that even though English is the language of international commerce, the native tongue of most of the world is not English.

Even in many European languages, there are characters that aren't used in English such as à, â, ç, é, è, ê, ë, î, ï, ô, û, ù, ü, and ÿ. Moving further afield, Russian and other East European languages use a Cyrillic alphabet. Then, of course, languages like Chinese and Japanese use characters with which we aren't even familiar. And some languages - such as Arabic and Hebrew - are further complicated by the fact that people write them right to left.

To deal with all of these languages, a system has developed to translate foreign characters into standard ASCII characters via an algorithm known as Punycode. These characters are then preceded by the prefix "xn--". This process can of course be reversed, and the name can be recoded.

The driving idea behind IDNs is that people want to use their own language on the internet, even if they know English. The basic investment concept behind IDNs is that as more and more people in non-English countries take to the internet, and as browsers support IDNs better, IDNs will be adopted more and more. It's time to get in early before the widespread adoption of IDNs, while the prices are still cheap.

If you are new to IDNs, it is best to try to specialize in one or two languages. If you already know the basics of a foreign language, that may be a good one to choose. Chinese and Russian are generally considered languages with a lot of IDN potential, because of their large populations and the so far comparatively low internet penetration in those countries. Japanese may also yield significant benefits given the country's wealth and technology savvy.

Also available are domains known as IDN.IDN. So far, we have been talking about the letters on the "left of the dot" being in a non-English language. But what about the letters on the "right of the dot"? Just as it's awkward for a native Chinese speaker to type "cars" into their browser, it is also awkward to type ".com."

The IDN world is moving quickly. The best way to keep up to date is to join and participate in a forum dedicated to IDNs, as most of the traditional domainer forums tend to neglect this topic. Your best choice for this is [IDN Forums](). I've found the level of discussion there quite high and there tends to be a very collegial atmosphere.

Conclusion: Buy for the End User

In today's marketplace (and tomorrow's), .com and is king. There are plenty of other investment options and more are expected to come... but none of these will compare in strength to the number this TLD.

Nonetheless, there are plenty of other options that hold value – but the key is to always have the end user in mind as well as their target market.

What does this mean?

This means that .info, .biz, .name, and .pro will always be limited because the average person doesn't understand that ".info is like .com, just different;" it means that .net is solid in many cases, but will always play second fiddle (or worse) to the .com; it means that a well established ccTLD will be great for local businesses and solid in value; and it means that speculative TLDs are just that – speculative.

The safest way to make money in domaining is to treat domain names like real estate. Names that have been proven in the past will only grow in value while relatively unknown speculative investments will require risk on your part.

You'll always be able to make some money on a new domain extension based on speculation, but the real money will be made with domains that hold the most value to the end user. I'm going to show you how to do your research, put a value on domains, monetize your site, and negotiate transactions so you can maximize your results.

The more you learn, the more calculated your risks will be – but if you're a beginner I'd recommend sticking with the meat and potatoes (.com and top ccTLDs) and save the gravy for later.

Chapter 5 - Domaining Niches

In This Chapter...

> - ✓ **Specializing Spells Opportunity**
> - ✓ **Geo Domains**
> - ✓ **Other Domain Niches**

Specializing Spells Opportunity

Most domainers, when they're starting out, think they'll do best if they're generalists. The common thought is that being open to the entire market will expose you to more great deals. But in domaining, like almost any other industry, you will actually make more money if you specialize in a set number of niches and master them.

Think about it. If you immersed yourself into a specific marketplace instead of being a generalist, you'd be able to...

- Value the domains you're interested in with unsurpassed accuracy.
- Easily differentiate the steals from the rip-offs.
- Build relationships with more buyers and sellers within your niche.
- Establish a reputation as somebody that can consistently deliver.

- Market the domains you own more effectively.
- Create a blueprint for "what works" in developing domains for your specific target market.

The opportunities are endless. People will trust you more simply because you have a specialized knowledge and they will happily buy from you and sell to you if they know you are a trustworthy individual.

Nonetheless, establishing a niche can be a bit scary and a little risky since you'll be cutting yourself off from a number of other opportunities. But the fact is… there are thousands upon thousands of domains available within every single niche, so opportunities will always be knocking on your door.

I'd recommend choosing 2-3 niches and learning them well. Start with one if you want and then move on to another. It's not a race, it's a business.

Choose Your Niches Wisely

In the same way you'd want to be careful in buying expensive domains with unproven TLD's (.mobi, .asia, etc), you'll want to choose your niches wisely as well.

There's a popular saying that says "don't put all your eggs in one basket." In domaining, there are enough proven niches that will never let you down. Just don't put all your eggs in the *wrong* basket. By doing due diligence and accurate research, you'll be fine.

Geo Domains

The term "Geo Domain" refers to domain names that are based on geography, such as neighbourhoods, cities, states, countries, or regions. Examples include BeverlyHills.com, Tokyo.com, Florida.com, Canada.com, and Caribbean.com.

As you can imagine, quality geographical domain names are very limited in number, especially if you want the .com or ccTLD. The great thing about geo domains is that they have instant name recognition and can be easily monetized. For example, Bahamas.com could either be used as a tourism-based website, a local news outlet, a source for local realty (or other) listings, or all of the above (and more)!

According to Sedo, "it is estimated that hundreds of millions of dollars in hotel sales result from visits to established and parked geo domain sites each year."

Geo Tips

1. **Development is Key**

Geo domains are ideal for investors looking for long term passive income. However, in order to get true value out of these domains, you must develop them. Once your site is established, it will receive better word of mouth advertising within the targeted geo area than any other domain could receive.

There is so much power in targeted traffic and by delivering content the consumer finds useful, your site name will spread like wildfire. You cannot beat free targeted traffic and very few domains can deliver this same result.

2. Think Small

People love websites that give them what they're looking for – and everybody loves local content. No matter what kind of mainstream content is available, people still like to know what's going on around them. It's the reason why national newspapers and local newspapers exist and it's the reason geodomains will always thrive.

> **Want to develop your website?** – See Chapter 11.

3. Unlimited Opportunities

The great thing about geo domains is that there are so many niches you can focus on.

You could choose to target California real estate, for instance, and slowly build your portfolio: SacramentoHomes.com, LAHomes.com, OrangeCountyHomes.com, SanDiegoHomes.com, etc.

Alternatively, you could focus on one area and develop domains for various industries, such as BostonMusic.com, BostonHotels.com, BostonCars.com, BostonNews.com, and BostonFood.com.

There aren't any rules to follow, only local markets to target. The potential for geodomains is huge!

4. Keywords Matter

If you are a consumer looking for a home in Toronto, Canada, which of the following 3 choices would you type in to the navigation menu or search engine: Homes.com, TorontoHomes.com, or Houses.com? Most likely, you'd search for TorontoHomes.com because it relates specifically to your needs.

If you're a small business owner in the real estate industry, then TorontoHomes.com would give you a very solid return on investment because of how directly it targets your key prospects.

Geo Techniques

5. Look Local

If you're not sure where to start, just look local. Don't worry about buying NewYork.com or Jamaica.com from the start; you need to start small before you can understand how to make things work on the large scale.

There are thousands of unregistered domains within your local area waiting to be registered. Additionally, you can buy many in the aftermarket as this niche has yet to be exploited.

6. Local Advertisers

The biggest advantage to geodomains is that your traffic is extremely targeted. Small businesses still depend on the printed yellow pages to pull in customers because the generic domains they own are difficult to find on the internet. Fortunately, geo domains cater to the local area and are great places for small businesses to advertise. You can even create a section for sortable business listings.

7. Plan for Success

The best way to get started with geo domains, like any other domain, is to develop a plan. Outline your exact intentions and create a sequence of actions that you will take to reach your goals.

If you ever get confused, don't give up. Instead, look to others that have done it before and understand the process. You will learn many tricks by communicating regularly with proven professionals through industry blogs and forums. There are numerous pitfalls to development, but if you stay active and communicate, you'll come out on top.

8. Don't Get Carried Away

The key to buying geo domains is to maintain a balance between domaining and developing. You should constantly be building your portfolio, but remember that they key to this niche is to generate streams of revenue. Don't get carried away registering thousands of names. Instead, find a few solid geo domains and develop them so you can purchase more high-end geo sites in the future.

Differentiate Yourself

Just because you choose a niche doesn't mean you have automatically separated yourself from the pack. How are you going to position your domains so they have more value? Always search for new opportunities to stand out. The richest domainers didn't get rich by following everybody else.

Other Niches

Adult Domains

Sex sells, which is why adult domains are a no-brainer. You can make a lot of money by running dating sites, adult video sites, or sites with other adult material. While it's not everybody's cup of tea, it has proven to be a lucrative investment online. Just don't tell your mother (or most anybody else, for that matter).

Gambling Domains

Gambling domains make up one of the most profitable niches on the internet. Domains that have anything to do with poker, sports betting, and Las Vegas have proven to be winners while thousands of fringe domains are still worth betting on. Although online gambling is considered illegal in the United States (and some other countries), domain name sales will continue to go through the roof as long as people continue to play.

Money & Banking Domains

There's always money to be had when you're dealing with money. Although this niche can be broken into several sub-niches, it's important to realize that they're all tied together. If you invest in credit card domains, stock market domains, get rich quick domains, banking domains, investment domains, or anything related then you're bound to see profitable results over time.

Health Domains

Earth's population is steadily growing and more people are gaining access to the internet, positioning this niche as a winner for years to come. People are already looking for health products online and several internet business owners have made millions selling alternative health products. As long as people are sick and tired of being sick and tired, health domains will continue to gain value.

Technology Domains
Domains within this niche can be easily commercialized, but rapidly outdated. TapePlayers.com might have been worth a lot ten years ago and MP3.com is probably worth a fortune right now. But what about the future? While there are always new investment opportunities for savvy investors, it is also a competitive niche that can be exhausting for anybody who continuously tries to lead the way.

Numeric Domains
In many Eastern countries, particularly China, for the same reason people use IDNs, people use numeric domains. While our alphabet is Western, numbers are universal, and a domain like 888.com has gravity and resonance across the globe. Numeric domains have been all the rage lately, and many a domainer has made a small fortune from these types of domains.

Honorable Mention
There are hundreds of niches that could prove to be profitable. Here are a few more to keep your eye on: career domains, travel domains, leisure domains, political domains, religious domains, food and drink domains, and educational domains.

Chapter 6 - How to Value Domains

In This Chapter...

- ✓ Wholesale and Retail Value
- ✓ Keeping Track of Reported Sales
- ✓ Popularity Matters
- ✓ Traffic is King
- ✓ Getting Down to Business
- ✓ Developed Domains
- ✓ Commercial Appraisals Don't Matter
- ✓ Ahead of the Trend
- ✓ 3 Letter, 4 Letter, and Brandable Names
- ✓ Useful Tools

The Importance of Understanding Value

To be a successful domainer you must know how to tell the difference between a great domain name and a bad one. But even more importantly, you need to know the difference between an overrated domain and an underrated one.

Let's face it, not every domain name can make you a million bucks. In fact, you'll probably never own a million dollar domain. But that's okay! There's still plenty of money to be had everywhere else in the industry.

In the same way that a real estate investor can make loads of money by carefully selecting undervalued houses, town homes, and condos – you too can make a lot of money by finding diamonds in the rough. As long as the demand for domains continues to grow, which it will, the value of your domain names will also continue to grow if you purchase wisely.

We all know that a single word commercially oriented generic term is worth a lot of money and a string of ten random letters is worthless…it's common sense. However, are you able to recognize a high-priced generic term as being a bargain or are you the person who dishes out thousands of dollars on speculation?

Speculation will always play a role in domaining, because it's our job as domainers to predict future growth. Nonetheless, there's much more to successful domaining than guesswork.

In this chapter I'm going to show you how to sort through the madness. There are millions of domain names out there, but a very few of them are actually worth anything.

The ability to effectively estimate the value of domains is the foundation of successful domaining. This chapter will teach you many important methods for appraising domain names before you buy them – learning this skill will save you a lot of money in the long run and improve your chances of striking gold time and time again.

Wholesale and Retail Value

One of the most important things to understand before you start tossing your money in the ring is the difference between wholesale and retail value.

- **Wholesale** is the price that a domainer will pay for a domain name.
- **Retail** is the price that an end user will pay for a domain name.

In almost every case there is a huge difference between the two. Domainers won't be able to monetize a domain nearly as well as an end user who already has a business in place. However, the Internet is full of domainers willing to sell at wholesale prices because it might be years before an end user is actually interested in their domain.

In fact, an end user will sometimes never come around to purchase mid to low quality domain names – opting instead to create their own domain name.

The wholesale prices will directly correlate with the perceived end user value of the domain and the likelihood that an end user will actually want it. The less chance of a developer coming along and purchasing at retail prices, the less money domainers will be willing to pay at wholesale.

What This Means to You

No matter what you're investing in, it's always best to buy low and sell high. Domaining is no different.

Many of the top domainers out there realize that wholesale prices on premium domain names will only be around for so long until an end user is ready to buy, which is why you see them holding on to thousands of domain names at any given time. They're willing to shell out big money (at wholesale prices) and pay the renewal fees year after year because they know there is bigger money to come.

Whether you're looking to buy expensive domains or cheap ones, the principle remains the same – buying at wholesale and selling at retail, although difficult, should be something you're always striving to do.

Keeping Track of Reported Sales

One of the best ways to estimate the value of a domain is to compare it to similar sales in the past. By looking at historical prices you'll get a good sense of the marketplace value.

My system for tracking sales includes:

1. **Domain Forums:** Forums are a great place to find out about recent domain sales and hear the opinions of active domainers. See the last chapter for a comprehensive list of all forums.

2. **Auction Results:** You'll quickly understand the domain market if you spend a little time each day, week, or at least month to skim over the most recent auction results. The best way of doing this is

to follow Ron Jackson's weekly sales report in **DNJournal.com**.

3. NameBio: The best tool around for finding and comparing domain sale prices. All you need to do is type in a general word or term that you're curious about, select your extension, and discover a history of sales results that compare to your criteria. You can even choose to refine your results by the number of words or letters in the domain name, or whether it has a hyphen in it or not.

Tracking industry sales won't only give you a grasp of how to value domain names, but it will also get you excited about purchasing your own names and making your own sales.

My one suggestion around this is to never act on impulse unless you are 100% sure about what you are buying. You wouldn't buy a house without taking a look through it, checking out the neighbourhood, and making sure it's valued correctly... so don't do that with your domains.

Popularity Matters

When you're looking to gauge the value of a domain, some of the most important indicators of value are those that can be measured. While there's always some speculation involved in domaining, impressive statistics and facts will greatly improve the value of a domain.

There are a number of questions to ask before purchasing a domain. How many people are searching for your keywords? How popular are your terms? What's the potential market for your end user? The answers to these questions will tell you a lot about a domains value.

Keyword Search Volume

Keyword search volume refers to the amount of times people are searching for a specific search term within a certain time period (day, week, month, or year).

The more people are searching, the more valuable a domain will be. If search engine volume is low for a specific term, then the domain name becomes less valuable.

There are a few tools that you can use to find out how much a keyword of interest is being used. The main ones are <u>Wordtracker</u>, <u>Google Adwords</u>, and <u>Keyword Discovery</u>. You can use any of these tools to find out how popular that keyword is and what terms are most often associated with it.

> **Warning:** Search engine volume does not equal search engine visitors. Just because somebody searches for "Example" doesn't mean they're going to click on the link for "Example.com".
>
> Nonetheless, high search engine volume is still valuable because you'll have a better chance of type-in traffic and more potential for Search Engine Optimization (SEO).

Keyword Frequency

Keyword frequency refers to the number of times a specific term is indexed by the search engines. A high keyword frequency (the more pages are indexed) is great for domain value while a low frequency means that the term is either 1) not worth using or 2) going to take a lot of effort to market.

Using the search engines to your advantage will help you distinguish what terms are important to a market and what ones are less valuable. We know that "basketball" is a much better term than "hoops" because more people are searching for it. While HoopStore.com might be catchy, BasketballStore.com will be easier to develop since it has 5-10 times the searches.

Nonetheless, checking for keyword frequency requires a lot of subjectivity since it's a test for how common a term is instead of how much money it can make. For instance – "and what" will pump out incredible results but AndWhat.com will be much more difficult to make money with than SportsCars.com, despite the fact that fewer pages contain the term.

Adsense Bids
You should always find out what advertisers are paying to bid on the keywords in a domain name.

The easiest way to do this is to type a domains keyword(s) into Google and run a search. There are a couple of things you can learn from the results:
1. More ads = more valuable
2. Quality ads = more valuable (I typed in "bike" and one ad was for a dating service...not good)

Google Adsense bids will tell you how much potential there is for domain monetization. If there are lots of ads for a domain's keywords then it will be easier to monetize as an affiliate marketplace or through pay-per-click (PPC) programs.

> **Roundup**
> **Demand –** <u>keyword search volume</u> measures how many people are searching for a keyword or phrase.
> **Common Use –** <u>keyword frequency</u> measures how many indexed websites pertain to a keyword or phrase.

Traffic is King

While keyword search volume, keyword frequency, and Adsense bids can help you understand demand, acceptance, and potential… nothing is more important than traffic.

Traffic refers to the amount of visitors to a domain and is best measured through the number of unique visitors per month.

Natural Traffic
Natural is any traffic that comes to a domain directly (without the help of a link), the most common form being type-in traffic.

A lot of internet users will type the keyword(s) of what they're looking for into the browser instead of going to a search engine. This type-in traffic is important in evaluating a domain's value because it shows whether or not the keyword is being used when people are searching for a particular product or service.

The more natural traffic a website has the more money it will make when the site is developed.

If 100 people are looking for pizza and 90 of them type-in Pizza.com, five type-in Pizza.net, and five type-in CheesePizza.com, then it quickly becomes obvious which domain name has more value.

> **What's Your Natural Traffic?**
> If you have a parked or hosted domain then you'll be able to find these numbers in your control panel or by using a statistics tracker such as Google Analytics.

Sample of Google Analytics

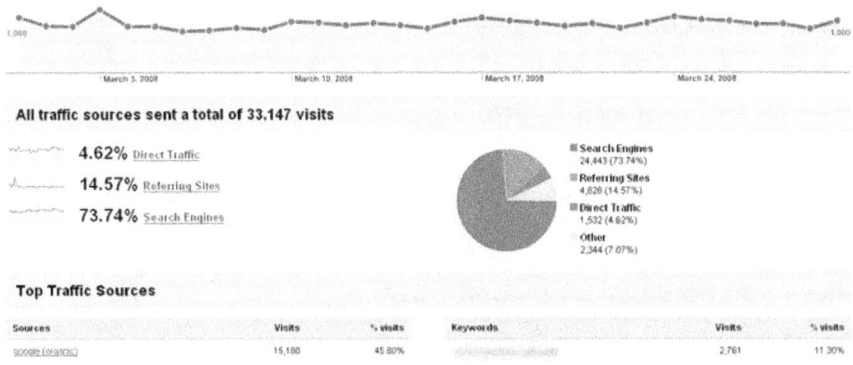

Link Traffic

Link traffic refers to any traffic that a domain gets through other websites including search engines.

Lots of link traffic increases the value of a domain name because it means the website is already established online and likely has some value to SEO.

When you're appraising a domain, it's important to have your facts straight. If you don't own the domain that you are appraising then you need to find out the statistics for yourself and double-check the accuracy. Quite a few people try to fake their traffic in order to increase the perceived value of their domain names.

Getting Down to Business

One of the most important factors in appraising a domain name is to evaluate whether or not it will be able to make money for the end user. While "casino" is one of the most profitable keywords available, there is a huge difference between "CasinoRoyale.com" and something goofy like "CasinoRacket.com" (yes, it was actually registered at one time).

People are constantly registering premium keywords with a misfit word because they feel it might still have value. If there's a fit that makes some sense without too much imagination then check it out – no harm done – but don't waste your time with the domains that have zero potential for monetization.

If somebody can't use a domain name to make money down the road, then it will never carry any real value. Here are some of the most tried and tested methods of seeing whether or not a domain name is worth any money.

Length (characters and words)

The shorter a domain name is, the more memorable it will be. People like short names and are constantly looking for them with type-in traffic. The end-user knows this as well and will understand that a shorter name is easier to market.

Domain name length can be measured in two ways: the number of letters or the number of words. In both cases, less is more – assuming it still passes the rest of your tests.

Pronounceable

To limit confusion, valuable domain names should be able to pass the radio test. Read the domain name out loud and answer the following questions:
- Was there a hyphen? (RadioWorld is better than Radio-World)
- Did I have to explain the number? (OneDollar or 1Dollar?)
- Did I have to explain the spelling? (Money4U, Money4You, or MoneyForYou)
- Is it a difficult word to spell?

If you answered "no" then the domain increases in value, if you answered "yes" it drops.

> **Standard is Better**
> You don't need to explain a domain name if it's the way people would normally type it in. Saying YouTube.com on the radio, for example, wouldn't cause many listeners to head to their computers and type in "uTube.com".

Branded

Visitors should know what they're arriving at when they type in a domain name. This can be accomplished through a well-marketed company name or a descriptive word/phrase.

If the target market has no idea what the website would have on it, then it plummets in value.

Grammar
If the domain doesn't sound right, it's probably because it's not right. Consider the difference of value between ToyStore.com, ToyStoring.com, StoreToys.com, and ToysStores.com.

When you are researching a domain name, you should ask the following questions:
- Would this sound better in singular form or plural?
- Is the suffix/prefix good, bad, or neutral?
- Does it make sense?

Industry Strength
Does the domain sound like something that could make money? Would it serve a purpose? Does the domain name describe or represent this purpose?

The more generic the term is the better. While there are many specific terms that carry significant value, they usually won't be as valuable as the generic term itself.

Example: Computers.com versus Laptops.com or HardDrives.com.

Prestige
Domain names have evolved to the point where an ordinary word with ".com" on the end of it is considered prestigious. Somebody surfing the web with the flu might type in "Pharmacy.com", believing in the back of their mind that the URL will take them to the website of a large pharmaceutical company.

While most regular English words have prestige in domaining, especially those that can be commercialized, it is also possible through marketing. A great example of this is Amazon.com.

Dot-Extension
As mentioned earlier, a domain's value is strongly attached to its TLD.

Developed Domains

If a website is already developed and pulling in monthly revenue, then you're paying for more than a domain – you're buying a business. This type of buying and selling isn't usually considered domaining, but I'll cover it anyways since you'll probably come across a number of developed domains for sale that might peak your interest.

It's important to note that you'll likely be paying retail prices for a developed domain instead of wholesale, but it still might be worth looking into.

Here are a few major factors you'll want to consider when appraising the value.

How developed is it?
If the website can run by itself without regular updates or a complete overhaul of the appearance, then the value increases significantly. If you need to rework everything from the start, then it's no different than buying a domain name and starting from scratch.

Since you're buying at retail prices, you want to make sure that the current set-up will be able to handle growth – because that's the only way you'll be able to increase the value in the long run.

Does it have steady traffic?
When buying a developed domain, you should look into the site history as far as possible. Has it always had steady traffic? How many years has it been around? The more established the website is in its market, the more valuable it will be. Incoming links, natural traffic, and Page Rank are all important factors.

Be careful of newly created domains with great numbers, it's getting easier for people to fake value and make money off a buyer that didn't do their research.

Does it generate revenue?
The going rate for revenue generating websites is the amount of money that it will make in the next 5+ years.

Also, the website is most valuable if it doesn't require much work on your part to manage or take to the next level.

Short, Brandable Names

Domainers these days seem to be crazy about short domains. The big question is whether there is any true value to these or if they're just going to be sold for wholesale for the next 5-10 years. If you're tired of seeing domains that don't seem to mean a thing sell for prices that say otherwise, then this chapter's for you.

3 Character Domains

Most domainers know that *3 letter* domains are extremely valuable because of the catchy acronyms that they can make, but what about those random *3 character* names? You know what I'm talking about... 1-m.com, b8q.com, 2cf.com, etc...

It all goes back to the basics – the domain is as only as valuable as others are willing to pay.

Right now the 3 character .com domains are selling like hotcakes to a starved crowd, but will this trend continue in the future? Will any of these find an end user? It's hard to tell, but it all depends on the combination of letters, numbers, and dashes.

Some letters are considered more valuable than others (s, m, d, t, vowels), while a few (x,y,q) are of little value. In the end, the random letters and numbers will have to mean something to someone.

4 Letter Domains

People say that 4 letter (LLLL) domains are brandable because they're short and sometimes easy to remember. But what kind of value should you put on such a name?

It all comes down to the meaning of the name. Something like CNHL has potential, because you can dream up the acronyms that it could represent: Canadian National Hockey League, Colorado Nurse & Hospital List, and whatever else. Other names you might not have as much luck.

Any 4 letter word that has meaning or can be easily marketed into having meaning is worth something in the long run and you might be able to find a great deal if the seller doesn't realize its potential. But you might also find yourself with a list of domain names that never sell for retail. It all depends on the market.

Don't Mistake "Brandable" For "Valuable"
Sellers will tell you all about their brandable domains that don't seem to mean anything at first glance, but be careful and decide for yourself.

Most of the time "brandable" only means that you'll get a name that will take thousands of dollars to advertise before your target market will ever see any meaning in it.

Think of Google.com. The domain was worthless until a company came along, chose the name for whatever reason, and then advertised it like mad. If it wasn't for them, you'd probably find Google.com selling for a couple hundred dollars somewhere.

The term "Google" didn't make the company, the company made the term.

Domain Value Diagram

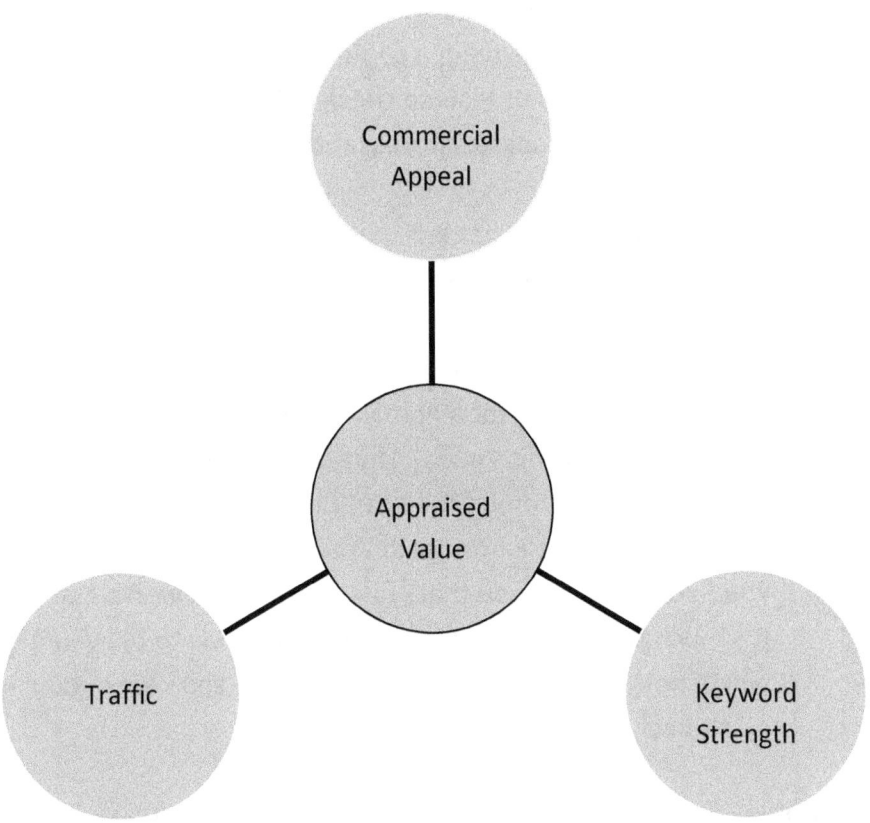

Commercial Appraisals Don't Matter

A number of websites – including Sedo, GoDaddy, and Moniker– are able to appraise your domain name if you're willing to pay the price.

A paid appraiser will run the domain name through a number of tests, much like you've learned in this book, and toss an estimate at you within a few days. But in my mind there are still two major problems:

1. They rarely have an actual person looking at the domain (that costs extra). Instead, a computer will run your domain through a number of tests to check if it has good letter combinations, strong keywords, and how long it is.

   Is that valuable? You bet it is, but why pay money for somebody else to appraise a domain if you can do it yourself in a matter of seconds or minutes?

2. When you're paying for a domain appraisal they have no reason to tell you "it's junk." They know that if they want to keep you as a customer, they can't lowball you on the estimate. Otherwise how would they rationalize charging you $20-$50 to tell you that your domains are worthless? It's much safer for them to estimate high than to tell you it's worth nothing – because it gives you hope and keeps you going back for more.

Expert domainers understand that commercial appraisals can be way off, high or low. In fact, most serious domainers know that *most* appraisals will be off. While every domainer and domain appraisal service will have their say on what a name is worth, the only two people that truly control the sale price are the buyer and the seller.

If the seller isn't willing to give a domain away for *x* amount of dollars, then that's the value it has to him. If the top buyer is only willing to pay *x* amount of dollars, then that's the value it has to him. Nobody else matters.

> **Peer Appraisals:** Most domain related forums have sections dedicated to appraisals. These can be helpful to somebody who knows little to nothing about domaining, but if you know how to estimate the value by yourself then there's no point in looking for help from others – in fact, it'll probably waste your

Free Appraisals

Aside from commercial appraisals, there is a free appraisal tool that is quite well known in the domaining community: Estibot.

Estibot can be helpful. It's not always right on the mark, but it generally understands whether a domain has good value or not. I like that it's not afraid of calling a domain worthless if that's the truth. It'll measure the domains keywords, frequency, Alexa rank, back links, PPC stats, extensions that the domain is registered, previous similar sales, etc… but it's still not human. I'd recommend this tool to any domainer, new or old, but it always comes with the caution: use it as a guideline, but nothing more.

Ahead of the Trend

As people continue to develop new technology, more markets will open up and certain domain names will rise in value. Think about what has happened in the past 20 years, the past 10, the past 5, or even the last 12 months.

Domains that are associated with potential trends are impossible to appraise because of the amount of speculation surrounding the industries and the keywords that will be associated with them.

However, if you think you've found gold then don't shy away because of uncertainty. While metrics play a large role in domaining, sometimes you might have a hunch that you simply can't ignore. If you think you're on to something big, thoroughly understand the potential, and can purchase domains for a good price then you should go for it – regardless of what the current statistics, trends, and marketplace may be.

Conclusion

While appraisal skills will always help you out in the long run, they aren't guaranteed to help you make money <u>all</u> the time. There a hundreds of factors that could change at any given time and greatly impact the value of your domain.

A new technology might sprout up, an old technology might die down, a new term might become popular, an old term might fade away, a business might fall in love with your domain name, or perhaps the end user you've been waiting for will never come out of hibernation.

You can only control what you can control, so as long as you consistently purchase domain names that offer a great value to your ideal end user, you'll have more wins than losses and earn a solid income in domaining.

Everything you've learned from this chapter should be used as guidelines for evaluating value. In the end, a domain is worth as much as somebody is willing to pay – no more or no less. You can analyze the statistics and learn the tricks all you want, but the true value will ultimately be decided upon by the end user.

> **What if the End User Isn't Willing to Pay Up?**
> Don't ever sell a domain if you don't feel you're getting a fair deal. You know what you paid for the domain, you know what the traffic is like, and you probably have a good idea about how much money can be made by the end user.
>
> Most buyers won't be the perfect fit for your domain; it's up

Chapter 7 - Buying Domains

In This Chapter...

- ✓ The Buyer's Advantage
- ✓ Quality vs. Quantity
- ✓ Where to Buy Domains
- ✓ Live Auctions
- ✓ Ensuring a Secure Transaction
- ✓ Buying Expired & Pre-Released Domains
- ✓ The Domain Deletion Cycle
- ✓ The Backorder Process
- ✓ Why Buy Expired Domains?
- ✓ Registration Fee Punts

The Buyer's Advantage

You'll note that I start this chapter with buying domains, rather than registering domains. The money in domaining is generally in domains that have already been registered, often for many years. You'll be buying your domains from other, rather than hand registering domains from scratch.

I can't emphasize this enough – buy your domains, don't hand register them.

Just to make sure you didn't miss this – buy, don't register domains. It is definitely enjoyable to hand register domains, and at the end of the chapter I'll give you some tips on how to do this. However, that should not be the main focus of your domaining.

As the market stands today, there are fewer buyers than there are sellers. If you're looking to get into domaining, there's no better time than now.

Well, that's not completely true: yesterday would have been better, last week would have been better, last month would have been better, a year ago would have been better, five years ago would have been even better, and if you had invested 10 years ago you'd have a great chance of being a millionaire. But still, as it stands right now – there's no better time to enter the market.

Domain names, especially valuable ones, are very limited in supply and only growing in demand. Fortunately for buyers, most domain owners aren't very patient and can't imagine waiting a year or two in order to make a profit. Most want money now… some even *need* money now!

Some domainers wait until the end of the month to make offers, hoping to come across somebody who is desperate to sell in order to pay rent. Others don't worry about the timing and figure they can find somebody desperate to sell no matter what day it is. Regardless of the situation, you'll always have the advantage if the seller needs the deal more than you do.

As a buyer, you can play the waiting game. If they don't want to sell you Example.com for the price you're willing to pay, then you can look elsewhere such as Sample.com, Possibility.com, or OtherOption.com.

While you have thousands of different domains you can invest in, the seller has a very limited amount of buyers to choose from. If they don't take your offer, they might have to wait another 6 months until they get another serious proposal.

Use this to your advantage, but make sure to remain professional. If they don't want to sell right now, you don't want to burn bridges that can be used in the future. Who knows… maybe they'll consider your offer a year down the road, maybe they'll give you a call when they put it up for auction, or maybe they'll offer to sell other domains to you.

Quality vs. Quantity

There are only two reasons you should buy a domain name:

1. To develop a website.
2. To resell it for a profit.

With that in mind, you should only be looking for domain names you are going to use for yourself or ones that you'll have a high chance of reselling to an end-user.

You've already learned how to value a domain, which is a great tool to help you search. The more generic a domain name is and the stronger keywords it contains, the more liquid it becomes.

You want to invest in domains with demand. Sure, you might need to pay a bit more right now, but you'll also make more down the road when you decide to sell. Chances are… if you buy a bunch of

$10 domains you'll be lucky to ever get your $10 back, but if you invest in a more valuable domain then it will only grow in value.

Many people struggle with one of two problems when it comes to buying domains:

1. Being overly optimistic
2. Being cheap

The optimistic buyer will see a "great deal" everywhere they look. While they might grab onto a steal here or there, they also end with loads of domain names that are very difficult to monetize or resell.

The cheap buyer will continuously purchase domains for less than $30, but have a difficult time spending any more. They don't dwell on things such as "return on investment," but find themselves busily searching for the needle in a haystack.

You, on the other hand, want to balance these problems. You want to be optimistic (but not overly so) and you also want to find great deals (without being cheap). This is the balance that every domainer should strive for.

Don't look to be a domain collector by picking up everything that catches your eye, but rather a domain investor by purchasing domains that make sense to your brain and bank account. It's better to have one great domain name than 100 worthless ones. While it will probably cost the same amount of money at the start, it will save you loads on registration fees one year later.

Quality sells...quantity smells.

Where to Buy Domains

Domain Marketplaces

Many sellers list their domain names on sites with a fixed sales price or asking for an offer. You'll have to sort through hundreds, thousands, and sometimes millions of names on a single website if you want to look over them all – but you're bound to find some great deals. Here are a few of the more popular places to find domains for sale:

- Sedo
- SnapNames
- Godaddy
- Afternic
- BuyDomains
- DomainNameSales

Auction/Offer Sites

Some of the domain marketplaces regularly run auctions of domains, where you can bid on domains for sale, and the highest bidder gets the domain. Some of the more popular auction houses are Sedo and Godaddy Auctions.

IMPORTANT NOTE: Buyers often get carried away bidding in these auctions. Just because you see more than one person bidding, does not mean that you should be too. Evaluate what you are willing to pay beforehand, and stick to it, regardless of what happens in the auction. Sometimes, not overpaying at an auction is the real win.

Expired and Pre-Released

This is discussed in detail later in this chapter and is often a decent way to pick up fairly priced domains.

Domain Forums

Some sellers avoid auction sites like the plague. You can find some great deals and make some valuable contacts by finding domains for sale in forums. Just make sure to protect yourself against theft (more on that later). See the final chapter of this book for a comprehensive list of domain forums.

Queries

You always have the option to approach a domain owner and check to see if they're interested in selling. The following tips and tools might be useful:

- <u>Internic Whois Search</u>: Type in a domain name and find out who owns it. This will help you get in touch with the person you want to buy from.
- *Use a Free Email:* Don't send a query using your business email address; you don't want the seller to know too much about you in case it affects their sale price.
- *Be Reasonable:* You don't have to offer right away, a casual email might peak a seller's interest. However, if you do want to send an offer, be careful in choosing your price. A low bid might offend the seller while a high bid might cost you more than what you needed to pay.

Note: *Buying* domains always refers to aftermarket purchases, as opposed to *registering* domains as we discussed in Chapter 2.

Buying Expired & Pre-Released Domains

Since domain names have to be renewed from time to time, owners who haven't done anything with their domain names often let them expire or accidentally allow them to slip away. In fact, thousands of domains expire every single day – some of which can be quite valuable.

A few years ago, one person let Quickly.com expire – a domain that *quickly* fetched over $45,000 when it went for bidding. In another high-end drop, Shoppers.com expired and was snapped up and sold by Pool.com for $166,000.

Gems like these are rare, but their stories prove they exist. Sure, you might not come across domains like this every week or even every year – and when you do they are often put up for auction to the highest bidder that placed a pre-order... but they *still* exist.

Sounds exciting, doesn't it? Of course, but it's also a lot of work, as you have to sort through a lot of junk to find domains worth buying. In March 2008, Frank Schilling told readers of his Seven Mile blog (no longer live on the internet):

> "In my 6 years of scanning expiring domain name lists I've found that only 7-12% of all names that expire mean anything to more than one person. The rest are such poor made-up quality that they have no resonance or gravity and they will likely never be looked up on whois, or typed into the browser by anyone other than the name's registrant.
>
> The other 88-93% of names are meaningful to the sole distinctive entity that registered them. They include

odd/trademarked strings, made up words, disjointed phrases. They are the trees in the forest, falling, that nobody is there to hear."

These days, the domains that do have value, however rare they may be, are more difficult to get a hold of than ever before. Registrars are grabbing hold of domains before they become available and offering pre-order registration to anybody that is interested.

The Domain Deletion Cycle

Step 1 - *Active*
Length: 1-10 yrs
Owner receives an email when the domain is ready to expire.

Step 2 – *Expired*
Length 1-45 days
Domain is expired, but the owner has option to renew or confirm deletion.

Step 3 – *RGP*
Length 30 days
Redemption Grace Period...Owner can still renew for a fee of almost $200.

Step 4 – *Deletion*
Length 5 days
Domain is deleted from the registry and cannot be renewed by the registrant.

Step 5 -*Available*
Length 1-45 days
Released

The Backorder Process

The backorder process is in place so everybody has an equal chance of getting the domain names they want. You can backorder any domain name, even registered ones, anytime until moments before it is released.

When a domain becomes available, dropcatcher services such as [Pool](), [SnapNames](), and [NameJet]() will attempt to register the domain on your behalf (and for other people who requested the domain) as soon as the domain is deleted from the registry. You could try to do this yourself, but you probably won't stand a chance of getting it at the drop since you'll be competing with avid domainers and large companies that have hundreds of servers searching the registry thousands of time per second to grab the domain name as soon as it expires.

If you really want a domain, you should use *all* these services to catch the expiring domain name. They'll only charge you if they get the domain, so you don't risk paying for a service that comes up empty. However, if others requested the same domain then you'll enter a short auction period to determine who gets to own the domain.

Why Buy Expired Domains?

A quality expired domain is normally a much better investment than a new registration because of the age factor. The earlier a domain was originally registered, the more likely it is to be valuable.

While it can be expensive to grab the domain if it goes to auction, it is often worth it if the value is there. Sure, 88-93% of the domains will be useless, but the others might be great!

> **Note:** You should still evaluate the domains as you would with any other purchase!

Registration Fee Punts

If you ask domainers what they think about registering new domains, you'll come across two schools of thought.

1. They're unregistered for a reason.
2. There's nothing to lose, except 10 measly bucks.

I know top domainers who register domains all the time. However, they have years of expertise under their belt, plus money to burn if their hand registrations do not work out.

Generally, I do not recommend that beginners make a lot of hand registrations. Wait until you've got some proven expertise and then you can make registration fee punts.

If you're determined to hand register domains, here's the basic method for success:

1. **Choose a niche.** I'd recommend a niche with commercial appeal.

2. **Quality domains.** Choose .com's. Ignore the other tld's and don't choose a domain with a dash or a number in it.

3. **Keyword tool.** Go to the Google Adwords Keyword Tool. Type in your keyword and click "get keyword ideas."

4. **Sort.** Sort your results by average search volume. This ensures that the most popular keywords are at the top of your list.

5. **Copy the results.** Click the "download all keywords" link at the bottom of the keyword list.

6. **Bulk domain check.** You then simply paste the results in a bulk keyword checker. You could use either GoDaddy or Moniker – they both work great. With either tool, you don't need to worry about deleting spaces or adding .com at the end.

7. **Choose domains.** You now have a list of keyword rich domains that are available. Go through the list and choose the best one(s) that are available and register them.

8. **Park (or Develop), Rinse and Repeat** (more on parking later).

Chapter 8 - Transferring Domains

In This Chapter...

- ✓ Overview
- ✓ Change of Account or Registrar Transfer
- ✓ Domain Transfer or Registrant Transfer
- ✓ Ensuring A Secure Transaction
- ✓ Escrow

Overview

You'll need to know how to transfer a domain if you want to participate in aftermarket activity (buying and selling of already owned domain names) or change registrars for whatever reason (poor service, save money, renew a domain, or to have all your domains at one place).

There are generally two different processes; I'll explain each one so that you can transfer your domains with ease.

Change of Account or Registrant Transfer

Transferring the ownership of the domain from one entity to another.

1. Log-in to your account.
2. Access your domain list.
3. Go to "account change" or "transfer domain" (depending on registrar).
4. Enter new owner details.
5. Complete the transfer request.

The registrar will send both parties an email notification regarding the initiated transfer and the new owner will usually receive security keys and other important transfer information. There will also be a set of steps outlined in the email that must be taken before the transfer is final...

1. New owner logs-in to account.
2. New owner goes to "pending changes" screen.
3. New owner enters security codes found in the email and completes the process.

Notes:
- Is initiated by the seller.
- Can be done anytime – from day one of ownership until the expiration date.
- Doesn't always imply the domain will be transferred to another registrar...just another owner.
- A transfer fee is rarely (but sometimes) charged.

Domain Transfer or Registrar Transfer

Transferring the domain from one registrar to another while maintaining ownership.

1. Log-in to your account at current registrar.
2. Remove registrar lock – usually found by going to your domain list, selecting the domain, and changing the status of the lock.

> **Note:** A lock is sometimes put in place to prevent unwanted transfers.

3. Log-in to your account at the registrar you're transferring to.
4. Access the domain transfer screen and initiate the transfer of your domain.

Note: You'll usually have to pay a fee to transfer domains, but can get better rates when you're transferring in bulk.

5. You'll receive an email explaining that a transfer has been initiated – the email is sent to the address you used at your original registrar.
6. Confirm the transfer from your original registrar.
7. Transfer is completed (although it might take a few hours to show).

Notes:
- Usually done with one owner, although you *can* transfer a domain to somebody else through this process (it would be initiated by the buyer).
- Cannot be done within 60 days of initial registration or within 7 days of expiration.
- Although it costs a small fee to transfer, a one-year registration extension is often included for free if you pay for a second year.

Ensuring a Secure Transaction

It's disappointing to have to add this section to this book, but unsecure transactions remain a problem in domaining. You'll come across hacked domains, banned domains, domains with fake traffic reports, trademarked domains, and domainers that will take your money and run. While domain transaction issues are rare, the problem *does* exist – so you need to be careful.

Here are five ways to make sure your domain purchases are smooth and secure:

1. **Do Your Research:** Find out all the information you can about the domain you're buying, especially if traffic and revenue streams play a role in the price. Don't trust screenshots or statistics without being able to verify them yourself. You should run the domain name through the evaluation methods I discussed in Chapter 5.

2. **Pay Attention to Reputation**: Most forums have a seller system in place where you can see a seller's trader rating. If they've been easy to deal with in the past, then you can trust them more than somebody with a low rating (or none whatsoever).

3. **Use Escrow**: If you're buying from an anonymous seller or somebody with a low rating then you should *always* use an escrow service. Most auction sites have their own escrow service in place, but Escrow.com is even better. Sure, it might be a hassle to pay the small fee, but if you're

spending a large amount of money on a domain then you'll be relieved to have it go through without any issues.

> Instead of using PayPal, you should use Escrow.com for sales over $300, unless you know the buyer well. You can also trust the escrow services at online marketplaces such as Sedo.

4. **Be Cautious**: If something seems fishy, it probably is. If you're ever uncomfortable with the way a transaction is being handled then you should report it to the auction site or domain forum where it originated.

5. **Get a Second Opinion**: Do you feel like somebody's taking advantage of you? Explain your situation at a forum and get other domainers' perspective. You shouldn't mention the domain you're trying to buy (or you'll have competition) or the person you're buying from (in case it's a misunderstanding), but definitely get help from others if you're unsure of the situation.

Standard Sales Process

In most transactions, the buyer will pay and then the seller will transfer the domain once they've received the money. This system favors the seller, so you need to go out of your way as a buyer to make sure the deal goes through as planned.

Chapter 9 - Selling Domains

In This Chapter...

- ✓ **Why Sell?**
- ✓ **Passive & Proactive Selling**
- ✓ **Selling to Other Domainers**
- ✓ **Selling to End Users**
- ✓ **Escrow**
- ✓ **What Not to Use**

Why Sell?

You can't earn a living in domaining unless you're able to sell your domains at some point in time. The whole purpose of domaining, like any investment, is to buy low and sell high.

If you have a domain that has peaked in value – with buzz in the news and a large amount of end users interested in it – then the only reason you would ever want to hold onto it is if you want to develop it yourself.

Selling domains is just as important as buying them. Sometimes you'll buy an undervalued domain and sell for the going rate to make a profit, other times you'll overpay for a domain and develop it so it's worth even more.

Passive & Proactive Selling

There are two main methods of making initial contact with a buyer...

Passive Selling: This is where you wait for buyers to contact you about the domain. While you may have to wait a while for something to happen, this is generally the best way of selling a domain since you know they want your domain – you won't have to worry about marketing or explaining the value. For the most part, high quality domains will receive much more attention than average ones.

Proactive Selling: This is where you advertise your domains for sale and contact buyers to see if they're interested. While this method will raise awareness and draw some attention, it will also put you in a weaker position to negotiate since people know you're looking to sell. Ideally, you'll be able to get a few buyers interested and have them compete with each other for the domain.

Selling to Other Domainers

When you're looking to sell, you'll notice it's much easier to sell to domainers than it is to end users. Domainers are actively searching for good names to add to their portfolio. End users, on the other hand, often only want domains they can actually develop.

If you're looking for a quick sell you should target domainers. There is no "*best place*" to sell your domain, but here are the most popular options:

Aftermarkets: You can list your domain on a number of sites where it will be exposed to thousands of potential wholesale buyers. You might even find a few end users searching for domains through these listings.

Most aftermarkets charge commissions for any domain that is sold – sometimes it is percentage based and other times it's a flat rate. Some auction sites also have premium listing services which will give your domain more exposure for a specified fee.

You'll want to make sure that you provide accurate information for buyers to research including your description, category, statistics, and anything else.

Sedo, SnapNames, Godaddy, Fabulous, Afternic, BuyDomains, NameJet, and Pool.

Forums: If you're looking to sell a domain fast, then forums are the way to go. Your domain will be exposed to a large amount of potential buyers – many of whom are serious domainers looking to build their portfolios.

There are several things to keep in mind if you want to have a successful transaction:

1. **Build a Reputation:** The more active you are in the forum, the more people will trust you and want to deal with you. If

you are a contributing member that others respect, you'll make a lot more money in the long run.

2. **Set Your Price**: You'll want to make sure you've evaluated your domain correctly before posting it for sale. If you ask for too much, you'll be laughed at – if you ask for too little, you'll miss out on extra money.

3. **Put the Domain Name in the Title**: If you want to catch people's attention with a good name, then put the domain name in the title of your post.

4. **Keep it Simple:** You don't need to tell the story behind your domain, just list the price and any information that might increase its value such as statistics, revenue, or ranking.

5. **Stand Firm:** If nobody is biting, don't continuously reduce your price – it cheapens your domain. If you're listing a domain for $1000, there's no point of reducing it to $900. If somebody is interested in buying then they'll inquire about the domain regardless of a slight price change.

6. **Bump When Necessary:** In active forums, a domain for sale can fall off the front page if nobody has recently responded to your thread. If you want to keep it in front of potential buyers, then you should comment on your thread whenever it drops out of sight. But make sure you don't do it too often (once a day is pushing it), because moderators and forum members don't appreciate it much.

7. **Pay Attention to Ratings**: Buyers will either have a good history of buying domains, bad history, or no history at all. If

they have poor ratings, don't bother trading with them and if they have no rating then you'll want to be very careful. Ideally, you'll sell to a trusted forum member and the transaction will run smoothly.

8. **Receive Before You Give:** Make sure the buyer has paid you before you transfer the domain to them...it'll save you a lot of hassle if something goes wrong.

A list of forums is included in the last chapter of this book.

Selling Multiple Domains?

If you're selling a high-valued domain, keep it by itself. However, if you have a large number of mediocre names then it's best to have them all listed in one post.

Selling to End Users

Selling to end users is typically a much longer process than selling at wholesale prices for two main reasons:
1. You're asking for more money.
2. There are fewer potential buyers.

If you're holding out for the perfect sale, you might have to wait years until you find it. However, there are a few ways you can chase the sale of your dreams...

Landing Page: End users will often go to the website they are interested in buying before they ever consider making an offer. If you're looking to sell your domain, put up something – a parked page or custom design - to let people know it's for sale. It is important that people can see right away that your domain is for sale, and know how to contact you about it.

Brokers: By hiring a professional broker to make the sale, you'll pay a premium fee for a premium service. Most domain brokers only deal with high-quality domains because of the work involved and the commission they'll receive, but they'll often find an end-user for the sale. If you're going to go this route, you should...
- Make sure the broker is well-connected in your niche with a history of strong sales.
- Ask if they require exclusivity or if you can approach other brokers as well.
- Clarify the commission fee and ask if you need to pay even if they don't sell the domain.
- Find out what strategies they'll use to sell the domain name.

As a beginner, the best way to find a personal broker is through forums or recommendations.

	Selling to Domainers	Selling to End Users
Number of Potential Buyers	Many	Few
Pricing Point	Wholesale	Retail
Timeline	Usually Fast	Often Slow
Difficulty	Easy	Moderate

What <u>Not</u> to Use

As with anything online, there are a number of things you need to watch out for in order to protect yourself against scams. Here are a few things that have caused domainers some headaches in the past:

Appraisals – As I've mentioned earlier, so-called professional appraisals are nothing more than a cash-grab by people or companies that know a little bit about domaining. If you understand how to value a domain by yourself, as discussed earlier in this book, then you should never need to pay for somebody's opinion.

Emotion – Okay, I probably just made you roll your eyes…but domain sales should be made with your mind, not your feelings. You shouldn't be selling your domains to get a rush, nor should you act on impulse if somebody offers you a certain amount of money for your portfolio. Think things through and make solid business decisions that don't just make sense for you today, but also dollars for tomorrow.

Chapter 10 - Negotiation

In This Chapter...

> ✓ Five Negotiation Strategies for Buying a Domain Name

Five Negotiating Strategies for Buying a Domain Name

Every once in a while you'll stumble across a domain name that immediately catches your interest. It might be developed, parked, or simply owned by somebody else. Two things are certain: you want the domain and you'll need to negotiate with the owner to buy it.

There's no perfect path to guarantee you'll get the domain for the price you desire, but there are several strategies that will improve your odds. There are entire books written on the subject of negotiation, but I've narrowed it all down to the five best strategies for buying a domain name. Here they are...

1. **Don't Act Too Interested:** Casually contact the domain owner to find out whether or not they're interested in selling their domain name. You should never sound as though you're ready to buy right now. By playing it cool

you'll keep the seller's expectations low, which also helps prevent the final sale price from overinflating.

A possible approach might look like this: "Hey *[First Name]*, I noticed you aren't currently using your domain *[www.website.com]*. Are you planning to develop it in the future?"

2. **Create Urgency:** A great way to avoid back and forth negotiations is to create a sense of urgency. There are a number of ways you can do this; something like this would work:

   "Hi *[First Name]*, I'm looking at a domain name for a *[Industry]* website. My boss has allowed me a budget of *[Price]* and given me until the *[Date]* to secure a suitable name – yours is one of the ones that made the short list. If you're interested in selling it for this price, please let me know as soon as possible." By creating a short-deadline approach, the seller may be compelled to agree to a lower price.

3. **Don't Get Suckered By a "Minimum":** When you're negotiating a deal, the seller will often state the least amount of money they'd be willing to accept for the domain. Don't fall for it – especially if it's more than you think it is worth.

   I've had a number of sellers agree to an offer that was only 65-75% of their minimum price – so it's *not* set in stone. Here's a great way to get this done: "Hey *[First Name]*, I'm sorry to hear that's the least you'll accept for the domain. I *came into this discussion with a list of 5 possible domains I'd be willing to buy for [75% of the Minimum]. I suppose I'll have to look at my other options. I wish you the best of luck in the future."*

4. **Use a Boss:** Once you have started negotiating for the domain, you can gain a significant amount of control by acting as though you're not in charge. A great way of doing this is to create an imaginary boss (or other authoritative figure) that makes the ultimate decision. It might not be the most honest way of negotiating, but it *does* improve your chances of getting a great deal.

   Example: *"Thanks for getting back to me. I just need to talk it over with my boss before I can give you an answer – but I'll try to have it for you by tomorrow."*

   This not only buys you a bit more time, but it also allows you to come back at them later and say your "boss" is only willing to pay **[less money]**. A good negotiator will want to speak with the boss instead of you, but you can explain to them that your boss wants you to sort things out but still wishes to have the final say.

5. **Don't Make the Seller Feel Abused:** Too many people lose out on great domain names because they are going for blood rather than a good deal. If the seller feels you're trying to negotiate with them for the sole purpose of getting the lowest deal possible, they'll be turned off and not want to sell to you (even if they don't have other options). If you offer $500 and the seller sounds interested,

going for less would only damage your chances of buying the domain.

You want to come across in a friendly manner while still working within a set budget. There's a fine line between negotiating for a fair price and disrespecting the seller with your offers – make sure you stay on the right side of it.

Five Negotiating Strategies for Selling a Domain Name

Most people believe the buyer has the "power position" when it comes to negotiating for domain names since most sellers aren't presented with many, if any, retail offers. However, if you understand your domain will only grow in value over time then you are the one with the upper hand.

Here are some negotiating strategies you can use when selling your domain...

1. **Be Willing to Negotiate:** Domaining is all about money. Sometimes a negotiation will take a matter of minutes and other times it can take months or years. When you're approached to sell your domain, you've got to be willing to negotiate if you're ever going to make the sale.

    When you're negotiating, look for ways you can add to the perceived value of the domain. Perhaps you own Example.com *and* Example.net – would they be interested in the bundle? By opening your mind to negotiations you'll make far more sales than if you have your price set in stone.

2. **Listen to the Buyer:** At the beginning of a negotiation, the most important thing you can do is listen. By carefully inspecting what the prospective buyer says in their approach, you can pick up hints that will tell you how much they value the domain and how serious they are about purchasing it.

   By listening carefully you can weed out the serious buyers from the crowd and deal only with people that will be able to meet your price expectations.

3. **Never Be The First to Name a Price:** This is one of the most difficult strategies to implement, but it will help you make a lot of money in the long run. When you're asked how much you want for the domain, stating a number will usually do one of two things:
   a. Low Price – You'll sell for less than you could have.
   b. High Price – You'll cause your potential buyer to roll their eyes and move on.

   "How much" is a high pressure question – you usually don't have any way to gauge whether or not the buyer is looking for a wholesale deal or able to pay retail. Instead of guessing a price without having anything to work with, you should try to find out more about the buyer. You can do this by asking "what's your budget?" or even telling them...
   "Technically, it's not for sale right now as I'm looking to develop the domain – although I'd be willing to consider if a convincing offer presented itself." This will put the ball back in their court.

4. **Ask For More Than You Expect to Get:** Unless an offer is much more than you expected, you should politely decline saying something like... "Sorry, but you'll have to do better than that." Just make sure you aren't rude or pushy when getting your point across.

   Most buyers will start with a lower price than they're ultimately willing to pay. Because of this, you should also play the game and ask for more than you're ultimately willing to accept. This not only allows you to raise the perceived value of the domain, but it also provides you with some room to negotiate – as you can slowly lower the price to make them feel like they're getting a good deal.

5. **Look for a Win-Win:** One of the biggest mistakes you can make when negotiating is to try and "win". It's not you against them, buyer versus seller. Instead, it's two people trying to find out what works best for both parties. If you get more attached to winning a deal than making a sale then you're going to miss out on some great opportunities.

   Keep your emotions in check even if the other person loses their cool. By leaving your pride at the door, you're more likely to "win" in the end.

Chapter 11 - Making Money Through Domain Parking

In This Chapter...

> ✓ **What is Domain Parking?**
> ✓ **How to Park Your Domains**
>   1. Select a Parking Company
>   2. Register
>   3. Select Keywords and a Template
>   4. Set the Domain Nameserver to the Parking Co.
>   5. Performance Testing

Domain Parking – The Basics

Why work hard to generate money when domain parking takes almost no effort and pays well?
Your choice: work on a domain to generate an income or NOT work on a domain and still generate an income. It's a difficult choice!

What is domain parking?
Domain parking is pretty simple, really. You let a parking company display ads on your domain. The parking company normally has a contract with Google or Yahoo! to use their ad feeds. A visitor to

your domain clicks on an ad, the advertiser pays Google or Yahoo!; Google or Yahoo! pay a share of the revenue to the parking company, who pays a share of the revenue to you.

Domain parking is one method of earning money from your undeveloped domains. It's sweet in that it involves comparatively little work compared with developing a website or selling domains, yet can provide a good income. It scales incredibly well, allowing you to profit from thousands of domains, whereas realistically no one could ever develop that many domains.

If you don't develop a website, your registrar is probably going to park your page anyways – but you won't see any of the revenue. While this might not be a big deal to somebody with only a handful of domains, a domainer with hundreds or thousands of quality domains will be missing out on a lot of extra money. The more visitors your parked page gets and the higher quality your keywords are...the more money you can make.

Despite this, many newcomers to domaining have a lot of misconceptions about domain parking. To help, this article covers some of the basics of domain parking.

> **Note**: Parking is for domain names with existing traffic...it doesn't *create* traffic.

Why Park?

The main reason to park a domain is to make money through advertisements. If you don't have a website developed, then domain parking allows you to take advantage of your traffic and make money off of advertisements and links.

Your parking provider will set your landing page up with a template (which you can usually customize) for a small commission-based fee. These templates often look very similar to a real website, causing visitors to click on the links out of curiosity or relevancy. These clicks quickly add up to money in the bank.

> **Did You Know?** The average dormant domain, according to TrafficParking, receives an average of 8 hits per month due to direct type-ins, miss-types, keywords, search engine placement, old links, or other reasons. While the average seems low, there are a lot of bad names out there. Some premium parked pages receive hundreds of visitors each day.
> *For information about the importance of traffic, head back to Chapter 5 and read "Traffic is King".

How to Park Your Domains

Any serious domainer will tell you there are many strategies for getting the most out of domain parking. There are many parking companies competing for your business – each with their pros and cons – and there are many ways to tweak your landing page for the best results. This section has everything you need to know to get started...

Step 1: Select a Parking Company

There are several companies out there offering parking services. I recommend trying out a few different companies at a time and comparing the results. Everybody has their own preference when it comes to navigation, templates, payouts, and extra features. The best way to find what works for your domains is through trial and error.

> **Note**: You might not meet the requirements of all domain parking companies. They often require a certain number of domains, restrict against adult domains, and put new registrants on a waiting list.

Here are some of the parking companies you should consider, as well as pictures of their standard templates:

DomainApps.com – The parked pages are auto-generated, making it convenient for beginners. Experienced domainers, on the other hand, complain about not having enough control for customizing keywords. Nonetheless, their navigation is easy to use and they pay-out twice per month, allowing you to buy domains (and park them) more often with the generated revenue.

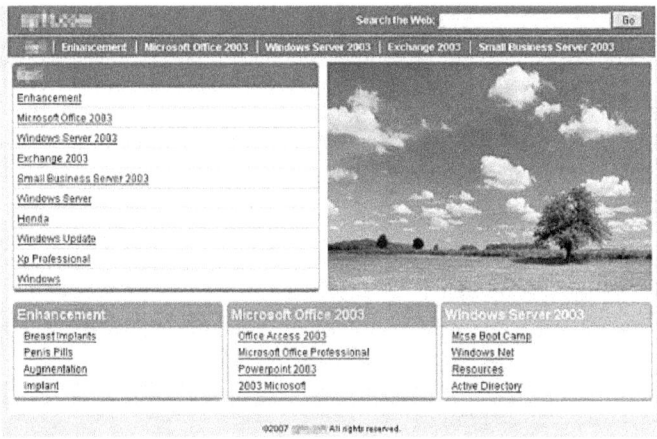

Sedo.com – Sedo is one of the largest parking companies out there and they are easy to get an account with. Since they also have a domain aftermarket, escrow service, and appraisal service you can be sure they'll be around for a long time. They're reliable and easy to use, although they are becoming so large that their landing pages hardly pass as real websites. Aside from their basic service, they also offer SedoPro, which has a higher payout and added options (although more restrictions). I generally recommend that people new to parking start with Sedo as they are the simplest parking company to set up with (plus you can list your domains for sale in their marketplace). You can use your results at Sedo as a baseline and then test other companies against them.

ParkingCrew.com – They have great looking landing pages that lead to more clicks, and their clicks tend to pay better for European traffic. You should check them out if you're having a tough time getting paid with another company. You won't be disappointed with their customer support and you'll also enjoy the fact that they support multiple extensions including many of the popular ccTLDs. Did I mention they have great templates?

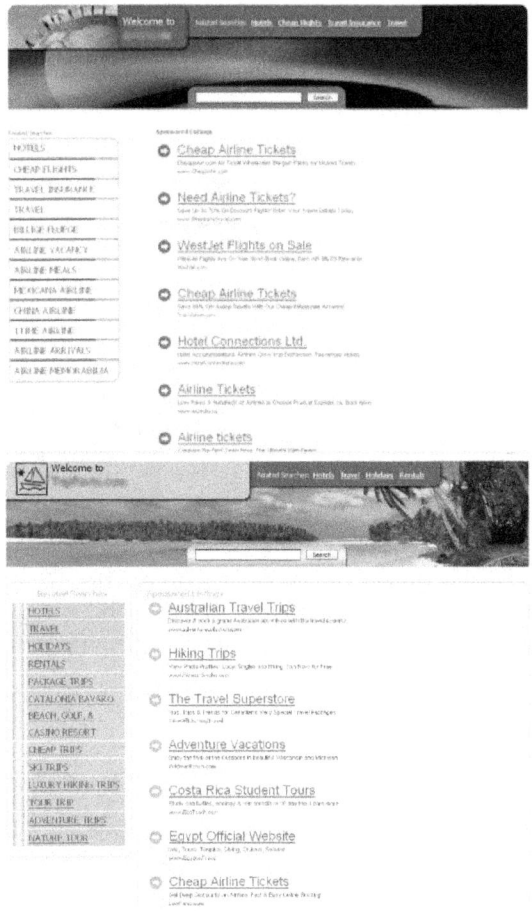

Fabulous.com – Fabulous has a very good looking template and control panel, although you'll need to meet their strict requirements if you want to use one (50+ domain names). They offer advanced reporting and are well known for their high payouts on adult and gambling names. The only complaint I've ever heard about Fabulous is that they tend to reject keywords. While this may annoy some, it will likely protect others. Nonetheless, if you have an adult or gambling domain then you cannot afford to ignore Fabulous.

DomainSponsor.com – They offer the closest thing to auto-optimization in the industry. While their system doesn't give you much control, it provides you with their recommended settings as soon as you submit your domain to their system. This is extremely useful for people with hundreds of domains. It's too bad their landing pages look so bland. Nonetheless, their conversion rates are solid – and that's all that really matters.

Bodis.com – They have the best system for stats I've seen, with near real-time analytics, and have released some crisp templates. However, their high click through rates and attractive style is marred by the fact they've had issues in the past with poor keyword optimization and database errors.

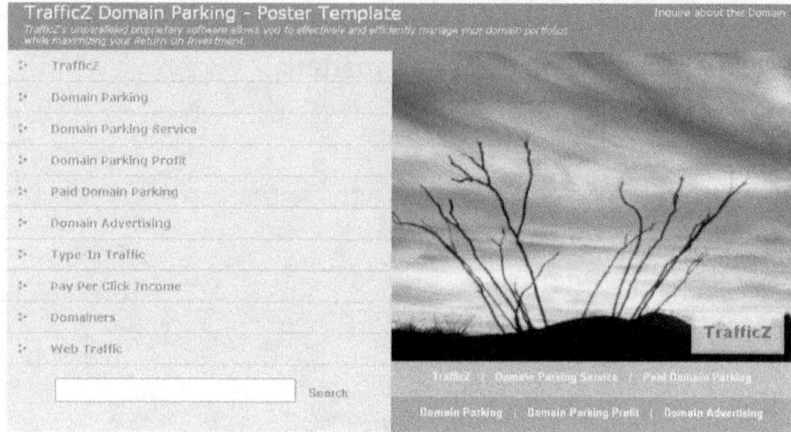

DomainNameSales.com – They are the latest and most exciting entrant to the domain parking industry. I tend to park my domain names here, as they seem to have the highest payouts. The catch, however, is that they are very selective about who they accept, generally only accepting large portfolios.

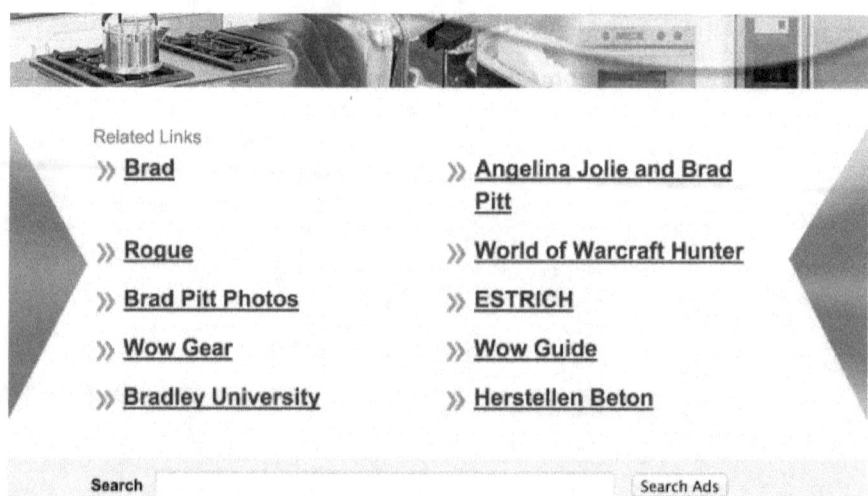

> More parking companies to consider: Skenzo, and DomainPower.

Step 2: Register

Once you've chosen which parking companies you are interested in, the next step is to register for the companies you've chosen. The registration process is a simple one and is well-explained at every company's website. You'll usually have to wait a few days while your application is processed, but after that you're in business.

Step 3: Select Keywords and a Template

Once you've been accepted, you'll have access to a control panel where you can adjust your settings. If your parking company allows you to have control over the page, then you need to be careful in selecting the right template and keywords that will suit your visitors.

A good keyword should be relevant to the topic of your domain (for a high click through rate - CTR) and easy to commercialize (for a high Cost Per Click - CPC). Here are a few things to consider so you can get the most out of your parked pages:

- **What Are Your Visitors Looking For?** – Your visitors arrived at your page looking for something. For a while, Cricket.com was a parked page with advertisements selling Cricket brand cell phones. I don't know who typically visited that site, but if they were looking for a cell phone then the links would be great. If most people were looking for information on the sport, however, they wouldn't useful in any way. *Note: information on the sport couldn't be commercialized as easily as the watch brand, so it probably offered lower CPC.

- **Do Your Ads Appeal to Your Audience?** – You need to carefully ensure that your wording grabs the visitor's attention and begs them to click. "Spaghetti Recipes" will outsell "Pasta" any day of the week and "Discount Flights" will always do better than "Airline Tickets." Make sure you find words and phrases that your visitors will click on.

- **Be Specific** – The more specific your terms are, the more likely your visitor will click on them – assuming it's what they were looking for. LeftyGolf.com should have ads pertaining to left-handed golfers, such as "left handed golf clubs", instead of random golf links (ex. "golf simulator" and "golf trips").

- **Choose Commercial Terms** – Regardless of your domain name, you should always look for terms that can be commercialized. An easy way to check if you've got a good term is to ask… "Does this term <u>directly</u> relate to something that can be bought?" "Hockey" is poor, but "Hockey Sticks", "Hockey Equipment", or "Hockey Tickets" are solid.

- **Use Multiple Terms** – A great way to improve the number of possible advertisements on your site is to use multiple related terms. For example, rather than just having "text messaging" you can try "text messaging SMS". If you want it to work then the terms must be compatible, but you'll usually be given a larger list of relevant ads by using this method.

- **The More the Merrier** – The more advertisers you have on your page, the better. You should have at least four ads, although you should aim for around 10.

You can use a tool like the Google Keyword Tool to find keywords that pay best in your domain's niche.

After you've figured out your keywords, you can go on to select your template. Every market is different, but color and design are always important factors for a parked domain.

If your visitors are looking to buy roses, then a rich red template would look nice. If your page is technology related, then blue or silver work great. Whatever industry you're in, you should have a general idea of its common colors. If not then test a few of them out, track the results, and choose the best converter.

Step 4: Set the Domain Nameserver to the Parking Company

In order for the parking process to go live, you'll need to redirect your domain to your parking company's nameservers. Once you register with a parking company, they'll provide you with two nameservers. Keep the numbers handy and follow this process to set up your domains for parking:

1. Log-in to the control panel at your domain's registrar.
2. Go to the area where you manage your domain.
3. Select the domain(s) you want to park and click "nameservers".
4. Read their information...
5. Put your parking company's nameservers into the spaces provided.
6. Click "okay" and...you're set!

> **Note**: If there's ever any doubt...follow the steps provided by your parking company. Their instructions should *always* overrule anything you read elsewhere, including this book.

Step 5: Performance Testing

If you're going to be serious about parking, you need to treat it like a business. The best marketing campaigns in real life are those that understand their market, have been tested and tweaked over and over again, and finally achieve success.

Just like real life, parking is a process and you shouldn't expect amazing results from the start. The more you get to know about your website visitors – who they are, where they're coming from, what they're looking for, and what they click on – the more money you'll be able to make.

There are a number of things you should keep an eye on to improve your income. The most important factors to keep testing out are your keywords, templates, and the parking company itself. Change your keywords, templates and parking company one at a time, and see how this affects your income earned.

My general rule of thumb is to try something out for at least one month before changing it. This allows it to have enough time to develop a reasonable sample size so I can compare it to statistics from the past.

If something isn't performing well, change it. But if something is working – and you've tested it enough to know it can't get *much* better – then let it be!

Note: If you are having a tough time testing, you can always get help from your account manager from the parking company. They want to keep your business, so you know they'll be willing to offer useful advice.

> ### Advertising Feeds
> Every parking company has a system set up where they provide you with advertisements from Google or Yahoo. While you often have control over sections of your parked page, paid advertisers will pay money to simply appear on your page – and ever more if they're clicked, allowing you to split the revenue with your parking company.

How Do I Get Traffic To My Parked Domains?

Unfortunately, this is the catch for many beginners starting out. Many domains, even domains with value, do not receive traffic on their own. While there is a temptation to figure out way to increase your domains' traffic, parking companies strictly prohibit you from doing this. Sending traffic to a parked page (for instance, through advertising, link building, etc.) is against all parking companies terms of service. The logic behind this is that Google and Yahoo are trying to get their ads in places where they don't already control the traffic – not recycling traffic that already exists. If a parking company find out that you have done this, they will cancel your account and not pay the money you have earned.

Parking is for domains that have pre-existing traffic (normally through direct navigation, mistypes, placement in the search engines, or old links). To make money from parking, you need to research and buy domain names that *already* have traffic. Don't just buy a domain name and then wonder how you can get traffic to it.

The key to success in making money from parking is owning domains that get natural traffic. Parking isn't about getting traffic to domains – it is about monetizing pre-existing traffic. To make money from parking, you need to research buying domains that already have traffic (by using various tools available, such as Alexa, Google external tool, etc).

How Do You Know Which Names Will Get Traffic?
Essentially, the answer to this question boils down to research, and trial and error. Before buying a domain name, you can inquire from the seller what traffic the domain receives. This is the most reliable method. However, note that the traffic stats can be games, so you should also do your due diligence.

You can do due diligence with Alexa, a tool that offers a "traffic rank" statistic about all websites. If a website receives any significant traffic, it will likely have an Alexa rank. You can also check the Google Keyword Tool to see if the domain itself (including the tld) gets domain searches.

Generally, most short and commercially oriented .com and cctlds receive at least a few type ins. However, I have also seen the odd domain in other extensions receive traffic, so do not discount those completely.

> **Note**: If a domain doesn't get traffic on its own, there is no sense in parking it. In fact, I would generally recommend against it, as parking a domain can increase the chances of a UDRP happening if the wrong ads appear on your domain.

Is Domain Parking Evil?

There is a lot of commentary in the blogosphere about domain parkers being evil, useless, lowlifes. Actually, come to think of it, there is a lot of commentary in the blogosphere about domainers being evil, useless, lowlifes. However, even many domainers claim that parked domains are useless and the general public does not like them.

My developed websites get a 5 to 10% click through rate on the ads and my parked pages get a 50% plus click through rate. From that, it seems to me that people are finding what they are looking for on parked pages.

The fact of the matter is – the traffic is already coming to the parked pages. You have a choice of showing your visitors nothing, or parking the domain and giving your visitors what they are looking for. How that can be evil is beyond me.

As well, parked pages provide more choice to consumers – they can choose from several companies offering what they want, versus just one company if a website were there.

In real life (is there such a thing?) people pay good money for publications like Autotrader, which are not much more than a bunch of ads. Is Autotrader evil? I certainly never heard anyone make that claim. Claiming that putting a version of that online makes it evil smacks of jealousy to me, more than anything else.

Chapter 12 - Domain Development

In This Chapter...

> ✓ Taking the Car Out of the Garage
> ✓ What Domains Should You Develop?
> ✓ Step-By-Step Development
> ✓ Monetizing a Developed Site
> ✓ Using Domain Development and Parking

Taking the Car Out of the Garage

So you've got a catchy name with end-user potential, but your parking service isn't sending you as much money as you anticipated. Don't worry, there is another solution.

Domain development, although more complicated than parking, has the ability to provide a stronger stream of income if you do things right. By putting up your own website, you'll create a flow of income that wasn't possible without development.

The development process consists of designing an effective layout, offering people a reason to visit, marketing your website, and making money off your visitors (or their actions).

Paying others to build a website for you can often cost a small fortune, but in this chapter I'm going to teach you how to effectively develop a domain on your own so you can create multiple streams of revenue online. You won't make as much money as parking in the short term – due to the initial costs and lack of advertisements – but once you have things up and running you'll experience a number of rewards that wouldn't have otherwise been possible.

What Domains Should You Develop?

If you're a domainer with hundreds of domain names, it can be quite difficult to choose what domains you want to develop and what ones you want to leave parked. This can be an even tougher call for a beginning domainer with a limited portfolio and less industry knowledge.

Here are a few things to consider:

- **Current Parking Revenue** – While you might hesitate to take your highest paying domain away from the parking service, it is *usually* the one with the most potential for development. Why? Because a high paying parked domain has end-user potential, a solid marketplace, and a large number of visitors that are looking for products or services.

- **Domain Value** – You're the one who bought your domains, so you're the one who knows their value. Much like parking revenue, a highly valued domain name has more potential to make money when developed.

- **Your Personal Interests** – Depending on what type of website you're starting, your personal interests will often play a role in whether or not the site will be a success. If you were a bachelor with a wedding site that needed a lot of content, you'd find it hard to deliver – causing your visitors to be unsatisfied. On the other hand, if you're a doctor with a great medical domain then the process would be much easier.

Step-By-Step Development

Starting a website can seem like a daunting task. Many people don't even know where to begin, but if you break the system down step-by-step it becomes a much more reasonable process. Here's your complete guide for developing your domain:

Vision: What do you want your site to be? Before you make any decisions regarding design or hosting, you should know your end goal. Do you want a blog wish fresh content added on a regular basis? Do you want a forum where visitors can take part in a community? How about a landing page to sell a customized information product? Perhaps you want a storefront to sell a number of affiliate products. There are dozens of options for you to choose from...follow your dream and put together a website you can be proud of.

Design: The options are endless. How do you want it coded – HTML/CSS, Flash, Javascript, CMS, PHP/MySQL, or something else? Do you want to make it yourself, use a service provider, or buy a template? Will your site be a simple landing page, ecommerce site, or a blog?

I wish I could show you an easy way to design your website, but there are too many options for me to even get started. One thing you should know: designing a website will cost you time and money.

WordPress Designing Guide

I've used WordPress to design all sorts of websites – static sites, blogs, landing pages, ecommerce storefronts, and more. While there are many of options out there, WordPress is worth trying out.

Here are a few resources to help you design your site:

- **Free WordPress Themes** – WordPress Themes, and TopWPThemes.
- **Premium WordPress Themes** – iThemes, SoloStream, and StudioPress.
- **Free Website Software** – Amaya, BlueFish, BlueVoda, DoodleKit, PageBreeze, and Yahoo! Site Builder.
- **Premium Website Software** – Adobe Dreamweaver.
- **Buy Templates** – TemplateMonster, TemplateWorld, and WebsiteTemplates.
- **Content Management Systems** – BitWeaver, Drupal, e107, Joomla, Mambo, and Plone.

Hosting: When your website is dormant or being parked, you don't need to pay for any hosting fees. But when you actually want to use your website, you'll have to pay to do so. Depending on your needs and traffic, you can pay anywhere from $5-15/month for web hosting for a simple website.

Graphics: Graphics and images will greatly enhance any website. If you're looking for a logo, banner design, or other customized graphics then I'd recommend posting a project for freelancers to bid on (such as Upwork). If you're just looking for some stock images or photos, check out iStockPhoto.

Content: For most websites, content is king. Without great content your visitors won't get what they're looking for, your prospects won't be interested in your products or services, and your advertisements won't convince people to click on them. If you're a good writer and understand your target market, then you're probably a safe person to take care of the grunt work. If not, you can hire a freelance web writer or copywriter to take care of this necessary task.

- Freelance Sites: <u>Upwork</u>, <u>Freelancer.com</u>, and <u>iFreelance</u>.

Search Engine Optimization: SEO includes anything that will help you climb up the ranks on Google, Yahoo, and other search engines. By using strong keywords, having people link to you, and creating relevant content you'll improve your website's search engine positioning and, in doing so, increase your traffic – ultimately leading to more sales, clicks on advertisements, and opportunity for growth.

Aaron Wall, a leading SEO expert, has released the ultimate source for everything SEO – <u>SEOBook</u> – and also updates <u>his blog</u> on a regular basis. You should also check out his <u>tools section</u> for a long list of resources that could benefit your website.

Advertising: A developed website is a lot like a business – when more people find out about your website, you'll become more successful. Advertising isn't a one-time thing; it's a constant process of getting in front of the right people at the right time. I recommend putting together a pay-per-click program, commenting actively on niche forums and blogs, sending out press releases, developing an e-newsletter, submitting articles to other websites (linking back to you), creating a blog, and more.

The most important thing in advertising is to *track your results*. By testing the different methods and discovering the varying returns on your investments, you'll uncover the most effective advertising methods for your site.

Monetizing a Developed Site

The Essentials

There are three main things you should look to increase when monetizing your website:

1. **Traffic:** Raising the number of visitors to your website will exponentially increase the amount of money you'll make from all your advertisement programs.

2. **Conversion:** By improving your conversion rates you can greatly increase your income without any additional traffic. The average untested and untrained conversion rate sits around 1%. By learning how to create powerful ads and place them in the right places, you could easily double that (a reasonable 2%) – which would also double your income!

3. **Diversification:** Another way to increase your earnings is to use additional advertising programs that apply to your target market. It's a well-known fact that the best way to make more money in business is to sell more to your existing audience.

The Key Strategies

Here are four great ways to make money on your developed website. By using these methods successfully at the same time, you'll experience a higher rate of income than ever before.

1. **Use Advertising Programs:** While Google Adsense is the most common program for monetizing your site, you should explore other possibilities as well.

2. **Find Sponsors:** If your website draws a targeted stream of traffic, other companies in your niche will want to advertise with you. You can sell banner ads or sidebar ads for products or websites apply to your market, but don't necessarily compete with what you have to offer.

3. **Use Affiliate Links:** By reviewing products – such as books, software, or training programs – that relate to your site's theme, you can generate income by using affiliate links. They often take a small amount of time to set up (going to the source and registering for their affiliate program), but the conversion rates are often impressive…especially when you give a glowing recommendation. You can also offer affiliate links in the resources section on your page and through banner ads.

4. **Create Products:** Once you've established yourself and have reliable traffic numbers, you can create a product and sell it through your website (assuming your site isn't a landing page, ecommerce site, or sales page). When people know and like you they'll see your products as valuable add-ons. A few options include eBooks, training courses, exclusive forums, classifieds sections, software programs, and merchandise.

Using Domain Development and Parking Together

While development certainly has its advantages over parking, it's also important to point out that it cannot and will not replace parking. Ever.

The key problem with the development trend is that most domainers underestimate the amount of time, money, and energy that goes into developing a successful site. It's actually quite substantial!

It's also important to recognize that developing a site is fairly trivial when looking at the big picture. While design and content creation may be quite costly, it is miniscule compared to everything else – marketing in particular. Marketing is a relentless, demanding, and never ending task that all developers must be aware of.

Given that most domainers are looking to develop large streams of passive income, development is not the best way to achieve this. Using domain development *and* parking together is!

While you can only develop and maintain a limited number of successful websites due to time constraints, there is no limit to the number of domains you can park and profit from. By using these strategies together, you can pick and choose the domains you feel capable of developing and use parking for the rest. Not only will this optimize your income, but it will also help you solidify your case against reverse domain name hijackers – since you can argue that you intend to develop *all your domains* at some point.

So, in short, development is great. But I don't think that development in any way replaces pure domaining, it's just a nice addition.

Chapter 13 - Domain Law

In This Chapter...

- ✓ Overview
- ✓ Trademark Issues
- ✓ Anti-Cybersquatting Consumer Protection Act
- ✓ UDRP and the Three-Pronged Test
- ✓ WIPO Arbitration and Mediation Center
- ✓ Cyber Bullying
- ✓ Reverse Domain Name Hijacking
- ✓ Domain Tasting
- ✓ Front Running (Domain Sniffing)
- ✓ Domain Security and Theft
- ✓ Setting Up a Company to Run Your Domain Business
- ✓ Tax Treatment of Domains

Overview

There has been a lot of news lately about domains that involve legal issues. The law regarding domains can be very complex and many domainers don't understand the consequences of this. To help you understand domain law a bit better, I've put this chapter together to outline the key issues within the industry. I know that you'll want to skip this chapter as it is not the most exciting subject matter, but knowing the basics of domain law is key to becoming a successful domainer.

You'll learn all about domain name disputes, trademark infringement, resolution policies, cyber bullying, domain tasting, front running, tax issues, and more. But before we get into the details, here are 13 important things to understand:

1. **The Contract Rules:** Most of the rights and obligations domain holders have are governed by the contract between the domain holder and the registrar. Naturally, since the registrar writes the contract, it is lopsided in favour of the registrar.

2. **Your Domain Can Be Shut Down**: Normally, the registrars' contract allows them to shut down your domain for whatever reason they choose. As well, most registrars' agreements don't require them to notify you in advance that they will be shutting your domain down.

3. **No Such Thing As Domain Ownership**: The registrars' agreements generally don't give domain holders any property or ownership rights in the domains they register - it's not really "your domain."

4. **US Law Overreaches International Boundaries:** Even if you live outside the United States, and your registrar is outside the United States, you may still be subject to the jurisdiction of the United States, simply because the registries for many TLDs are located in the United States. In short, if you are doing anything controversial with your domain, avoid any and every connection with the US, or choose a gtld that is

not based in the United States.

5. **Generics Can Be Trademarks:** Just because your domain is a generic word doesn't mean that it is not infringing a trademark. An "apple" is more than just a fruit. This is particularly important when parking your domain. You need to be very careful about the ads that appear on a parked domain.

6. **Registrars Will Park Your Domains**: If you don't change your nameservers when you register a domain, then chances are that your registrar will put up its own parking page. The registrar collects any revenue earned from the parking page. But if you find yourself in an UDRP due to ads from the registrar's parking page, you're the one who has to face the music, not the registrar.

7. **Record Keeping:** Keep good records of all your domain registrations, including any emails sent by your registrar. If there are ever any legal problems, there is a good chance you will need these.

8. **Private Whois:** If you use the private whois service offered by your registrar, it may be difficult to prove your right to a domain.

9. **Accurate Whois.** Don't use incorrect whois information on any domain of value. Your registrar can suspend your domain if you do this.

10. **Front Running:** For reasons I'll discuss later in this chapter – if you find a good domain name, register it right away. Rush

through the checkout process as quickly as possible.

11. **Hijacking:** If your domain gets hijacked, a lot of registrars won't help. Make sure you hold your domains with a registrar who takes security seriously.

12. **Most Registrars Aren't Helpful:** You can't expect much from your registrar, especially in legal matters. You pay them $9 or $10 per year for your domain; how much effort are they going to put in for that amount of money?

13. **Not Much Legal Protection:** Scammers are everywhere. In practical terms, there is little the law can do to help you if you are scammed. While it may be a theoretical possibility that the law can help, the international nature of domain names plus the high costs of legal proceedings in comparison to the value of most domains means that in practical terms, there is little you can do if something goes wrong.

So, if you're a domainer, before you start talking about your "rights" you might as well realize you don't have that many! Play it safe with your domains.

> Please note that nothing in this chapter should be considered professional advice. Instead, the material is only intended to be interpreted as potential concepts for domainers interested in protecting their rights in domain names.

Trademark Issues

People who have never traded in domains before instinctually think that one of the best domaining strategies is simply to buy up trademarked names and then hold out for a big payday when the company who owns the trademark wants to use it. Experienced domainers are not so naive as to think that buying Starbucks.com or Comcast.net before the actual company gets it is a viable business strategy. That said, there is a lot of gray area when it comes to domain name trademark issues, and knowing what the law is can help save you some money and a legal headache.

Major problems can arise when you have a domain name that is "confusingly similar" to another company's name, product, or service. In fact, many big-time lawsuits have been filed because of trademark issues. The best advice regarding trademark domains...DON'T TOUCH THEM!

In 2007 one cybersquatter, JP Vazquez, got hit with a lawsuit from Dell for having over 1100 domains that were confusingly similar to Dell's various trademarks. [via Washington Post]

While NBABasketball.com, GoogleResources.com, and MacSoftwareStore.com might have good traffic and offer great opportunities for monetization, there is way too much risk involved in purchasing these names regardless of how cheap you can get them.

What if You Already Have a Domain that Infringes on a Trademark?

Whatever you do, do not use the domain for anything that could be considered "bad faith" – such as benefitting by the confusion in any way. Often, the best decision would be to delete the domain.

However, some people choose to hold on to trademark domains for whatever reason. Perhaps you've chosen this path or maybe you don't even realize you own this kind of domain...

...If this is the case, the company or individual that registered the trademark will eventually have their attorney contact you with a Cease and Desist order – usually asking you to transfer the ownership of the domain to them for free.

If you believe you have rights to the domain (perhaps you registered it before the trademark was ever issued) then you should seek an experienced trademark attorney for advice.

> **Trademark Resources**
> If you need more information about trademarks, you should check out the website for the United States Patent and Trademark Offices as well as GGMark.

Anti-Cybersquatting Consumer Protection Act (ACPA)

In 1999, a new US federal law, the Anti-Cybersquatting Consumer Protection Act (ACPA), took effect with the intention of giving trademark owners legal rights against those who obtain domain names in "bad faith".

ACPA applies to cases where somebody...

1. Has a bad faith intent to profit from a domain name and/or
2. Obtained a domain name that is identical, confusingly similar, or dilutive of certain trademarks. The trademark does not have to be registered.

What is "Bad Faith"?
Bad faith is a legal concept that gives consideration not only to the legal rights of those involved, but also the motives of each party. A court is likely to find the domain name registrant has acted in bad faith if he or she has...

1. Tried to divert customers from a trademark owner's website to another for commercial gain.
2. Attempted to sell the domain name for a profit to either the trademark owner or somebody else without ever using it or having the intention of using it.
3. Provided false or misleading information when applying for registration.
4. Registered a number of names identical or similar to trademarks.

Bad faith intent will not be found if the court determines the person was going to use the domain name for a fair or otherwise lawful use.

UDRP and the Three-Pronged Test

Introduced in 1999, the Uniform Domain Name Dispute Resolution Policy (UDRP) is a quick and cost effective dispute resolution procedure. The UDRP defines how disputes over domain-name registrations are resolved for all the global top-level domains (and even most country's cctlds have dispute resolution provisions that are similar to the UDRP). Their policy is the authority on issues regarding claims of abusive, bad faith registration of someone else's trademark.

For a complainant to file a dispute against you or your registration of a domain, they must prove that three elements are present:

1. Your domain is identical or confusingly similar to a trademark or service mark in which the complainant has rights; and
2. You have no rights or legitimate interests in respect of the domain name; and
3. Your domain name has been registered and is being used in bad faith.

Proving one or two of these elements is not good enough for a dispute to go through, *all three MUST* be present. For a full copy of the UDRP, click here.

While the three prong rule is succinct on paper, in practice, it is far from straightforward. In particular, there is no clear definition of "no legitimate interest" nor "bad faith." Blatant cybersquatting or typosquatting is clearly illegal under the three part test; such as buying "www.Gooogle.com" and sending Google an email saying that you're going to put up porn on the site if they don't buy it from you for $10,000,000. But for less clear cases, such as whether holding "www.Googles.com" is a violation of Google's trademark, the UDRP three-prong test provides little guidance.

It's also important to keep in mind that just because a trademark isn't formally registered doesn't mean it doesn't exist. Trademarks can arise both through registration and through use. Trademarks that arise through use can equally be enforced in the US and in most countries (though not China) against people trying to cash in by using a confusingly similar name.

How to Stay Out of Trouble?

Never register a domain in the name of a known existing trademark. The days when cybersquatting was a viable business plan are long gone, and attempting to do so now is just going to cost you time and money. Make sure to check online for public trademarks, but know that any search you make is likely to provide you with only a partial view of the existing trademarks.

Always remember that just because a company's trademark is a part of your domain name does not mean you are necessarily in violation of that company's trademark rights. There are a number of exceptions including fair use, parody, non-commercial use, and non-competing use that may apply. In addition, trademarks are not universal, so the fact that the company holds a trademark in one area does not mean that their trademark necessarily applies to your domain.

Consider that many large companies overstate their trademark claims as a matter of policy. If you are a domainer with a lot of holdings, be prepared for overzealous C&D letters claiming that anything remotely close to their trademark is in violation of the law.

> **ACPA or UDRP?**
> While the UDRP process makes the most sense because of the low-cost involved and opportunity to avoid legal fees, it's sometimes disappointing how unpredictable the decisions can be. ACPA is certainly the more consistent process, but I don't know many people who want to spend thousands on a court case when these issues can be settled in more reasonable ways.

WIPO Arbitration and Mediation Center

The World Intellectual Property Organization (WIPO) Arbitration and Mediation Center was the first accredited ICANN dispute resolution provider and is well-recognized for being the most widely used UDRP provider in the world.

Other providers include:
- Asian Domain Name Dispute Resolution Center (ADNDRC)
- The National Arbitration Forum (NAF)
- The Czech Arbitration Court (CAC)

Cyber Bullying

While many businesses have legitimate reasons to issue Cease and Desist letters, others are trying to push small-time domainers around.

> In 1999, Lilly Industries – a company with a stain remover called *Goof Off* – threatened a lawsuit against Rick Schwartz, owner of GoofOff.com, claiming the domain should be theirs by rights.
>
> Schwartz, an icon in the domaining industry, was using Goofoff.com as an entertainment and travel site at the time – a far fetch from cybersquatting. Schwartz was so outraged at the bullying tactics that he decided to sue the company instead.
>
> *"According to Webster's, a 'Goof off' is a noun that means a person that wastes time or avoids work; a shirker. As such, Goofoff.com is being used quite appropriately,"* said Schwartz at the time. *"These 'corporate bullies' intimidate small firms and individuals into relinquishing domains through the threat of litigation despite the fact that they have no legal rights to the domain."* [via TheRegister.co.uk]

Lilly Industries isn't alone in the world of cyber bullying. There are many companies that know the threat of a lawsuit is enough to scare a smaller business away from the domain. They don't even need to win the case in order to obtain the domain; they just need to threaten action to make it so the domain registrant forfeits the domain in favor of paying thousands of dollars in legal fees.

> In 2007, SnapNames.com – a popular domain backordering service provider – bullied SwapNames Incorporated into

giving up their domain name SwapNames.com. According to SnapNames.com, because the domain was only one letter different they considered it to be "confusingly similar" to their own.

While SwapNames certainly had a strong case of defence, it chose to forfeit the domain and move on with business under a new identity.

"Even though we are absolutely certain that the allegation is baseless; we do not have the finances to hire an attorney to defend our case in court. As far as we know, a descriptive and generic phrase such as "swap names" cannot be infringing in anyway. However, to defend the lawsuit will certainly bankrupt our company, just from the hefty legal expenses." [via [DomainNameNews](#)]

The domainer's only defence? Avoid stepping on any toes, especially if they belong to a person with a significantly larger bank account than your own.

Reverse Domain Name Hijacking

Much like (and often the same thing as) cyber bullying, reverse domain name hijacking is the practice of unfairly attempting to unseat domain name registrants by accusing them of violating weak or non-existent trademarks related to the domain name – or in some cases attempting to claim trademark superiority.

With the recent onslaught of Cease and Desist letters, reverse domain name hijacking has become a reliable defence for registrants who feel they have valid rights to the domain and that they are not unreasonably infringing on any trademarks.

Front Running (Domain Sniffing)

Front running occurs when a person monitors the actions of somebody else who is planning to buy a domain name, and then the first person registers it before the second. "I had a really great domain name idea, which was available when I searched through the registrar, but then five minutes later when I went to buy the name it was gone." Anyone who has been in domaining for more than a month has heard dozens of versions of that same story.

While it seems common sense that somebody would register a great domain if they knew others were looking for it and it was still available, front running becomes particularly controversial with the involvement of domain registrars.

Evidence has surfaced over the past years that a number of registrars are tracking the domain name searches on their systems and registering any domain that isn't immediately purchased. This allows the registrar to taste it for the 5 day grace period and also grants them the sole resale rights for the domain unless they choose to release it.

While the issue is sure to continue receiving criticism and possibly action from ICANN, you can't control much of that. One thing you can do, however, is be careful about which registrar you use to search for available domains.

Domain Security and Theft

Since domains are on the internet, they are as susceptible to theft as anything else online. As always, however, there are certain precautions you can take to keep out of trouble.

Here are a few tips for avoiding domain theft:

1. **Be Careful With Transactions**: We discussed domain transactions earlier, but this should be re-emphasized. Don't give out more information than you need and don't trust anybody more than you should. Take every precaution to remain as anonymous as the system allows you to be.

2. **Keep Your Domains Safe**: Make sure your domains are with a registrar that cares about domain security - Moniker and Fabulous are the two that everyone states are good in this regard. Apparently, neither registrar has ever had a domain stolen.

3. **Don't Use Free Email Accounts:** Free email accounts should not be used as the contact for your domains. The normal way that a thief gets control of a domain is by getting control of the email account of the administrative contact. Free email accounts are generally easier to hack than ones that you control.

Setting up a Company to Run Your Domain Business

What Legal Entity Should I Use?

Many domainers started out with nothing more than a few hundred dollars and an internet connection. So when it came to spending time and money to create a separate legal entity, many domainers just chose to operate under the default legal form DBA, which offers no legal protection. Even now, many domainers remain confused about whether they need to form a separate entity, which one they should choose, and why. Unlike other issues in domaining law, thankfully the laws surrounding entity types are pretty straightforward.

What is the Law?
When you own domains yourself (as opposed to through a legal entity) your personal assets, such as your personal savings, car, etc., are at risk if something goes wrong. So for instance, if you're being sued for a trademark violation and you lose the case, you could lose your personal assets as well as the company assets. Suffice it to say, forming a separate legal entity for your domaining company is important.

There are a few major options when deciding which entity to form, each of which has its drawbacks.

C-Corporation:
Most Fortune 500 companies are C-Corp's, which leads many new domainers to believe that it is the right choice for them. For domainers, C-Corps just mean an extra layer of 15% taxes, and probably aren't desirable unless your company is planning on going public (a.k.a. having an IPO) in the very near future.

General Partnership:
There's two of you in the company and you call yourselves partners, so the logical choice is to form a partnership, right?

Wrong. A general partnership is the ugly stepchild to the LLC and S-Corp, because in a general partnership there has to be one person or entity designated as the general partner. Whoever that is doesn't get limited liability. Thus, if your company got sued and it was formed as a general partnership, the general partners' personal assets (personal savings, car, etc.) would all be included in the pot of money that creditors or the people that sue you can get to.

S-Corp:
Given that a General Partnership or C-Corp aren't likely the best choice for your domaining company, the real choice is between an S-Corp and an LLC. Both offer limited liability to all the members (unlike a General Partnership) and neither has an extra layer of tax (unlike a C-Corporation). S-Corp's are advantageous because they allow the owners to allocate part of the company income to a salary and part as a profit distribution, whereas an LLC treats all company profits as salary. The distinction is important because a domainer's salary is subject to a self-employment tax, whereas passive income isn't. So if you think your company is going to make enough money that it would exceed a reasonable salary for you, and if you are already planning on having employees, which means you're already going to prepare payroll tax returns, then the S-Corp may be the way to go.

Limited Liability Company (LLC):
LLC's are the newest legal entities and they provide an advantage over S-Corp's because you can allocate profits in your company differently than you allocate ownership interests. That means that if you want to keep 100% ownership of your company but give your employees a share in the profits you can with an LLC (but can't with an S-Corp). They also have the advantage of requiring virtually no

paperwork or technicalities like an annual meeting of the shareholders to remain in compliance. The downside is that all of your company profits are treated as a salary, which means you'll be paying more in self-employment tax than you would under an S-Corp. For most one or two person domaining companies, LLC's are the way to go. They offer as good of liability protection as any other form, have low tax obligations, and give you some flexibility in how you want to structure profits.

How to Stay Out of Trouble?
Never form a C-Corporation or Limited Liability Partnership unless you have good reason to do so and have checked with an accountant first. The administrative, legal, and tax problems from a small domaining company's perspective make these pretty terrible options for most.

Always write up a reasonable long-term projection for your business before choosing your entity. Deciding which legal form is best for your company depends not only upon your current situation, but also on the future, and getting it right early is a lot better than trying to fix things later.

Consider that the choice between an S-Corp and an LLC is a technical one which depends a lot on whether you plan to have other employees or not. That means that before you decide between the two options you should figure out whether the people that work for you are considered "independent contractors" or "employees" (discussed below).

What State to Legally Form Your Company In

If you poke around the list of Fortune 500 companies, you'll find that the vast majority are incorporated in Delaware or Nevada. The reason why, is that these states have developed a set of laws which are predictable and which tend to favor corporations and their officers over the people suing them. By contrast, some states lean the other way and tend to favor plaintiffs.

What is the Law?
You can form your company in any state you want, but wherever you do it, you'll need to have a mailing address. So if you decide you want to take advantage of the pro-business laws in Delaware, you'll need to cough up about $300 a year in order to pay somebody to be your "registered agent" in Delaware. There are online services which do this, but in essence it just means that you're paying somebody in Delaware to accept mail on your behalf if the State of Delaware ever needs to contact you (such as when somebody is suing you).

When choosing between Delaware and Nevada, there is very little difference. Delaware has been the historical choice for corporations, but to get in on the act Nevada simply adopted all of Delaware's corporation law, plus it provided the added bonus of allowing anonymous shareholders, officers and directors by not requiring that corporate information be public record. But if you're not interested in remaining anonymous, there's virtually no difference between Delaware and Nevada.

A common rumor is that you can avoid taxes by incorporating in Delaware or Nevada. States tax businesses at different rates; unfortunately, however, your state taxes aren't tied to where you're incorporated, but where you operate. So whether you choose to incorporate in Delaware, Nevada, or any other place, you'll still be paying your home state's taxes for any money you make.

How to Stay Out of Trouble?
Never attempt to avoid taxes by forming your company in another state. It simply doesn't work, despite the fact that seemingly everyone who isn't an accountant or lawyer thinks it does.

Always read up on what legal commentators are saying about the corporate laws in your home state before forming your company. Some states are particularly archaic (e.g. Pennsylvania) and you should probably avoid forming there, despite the added cost.

Consider that a state's corporate laws are determined by a variety of factors, so there's no way of predicting absent research which home states are corporate friendly and which aren't. Some states with a historically strong union presence or states with no real history of any corporations at all tend to be especially bad because the plaintiff's lawyers bar is so strong relative to the defense lawyer's bar. That said, the only real way to know how your state stands is to check with a local corporate lawyer.

Piercing the Corporate Veil

The primary reason for forming a legal entity and not simply operating your business as a DBA is for limited liability protection. But you only get that protection if the law recognizes your legal entity as separate from you or the other officers in your company. Thankfully, the law governing whether to disregard your separate legal entity, also known as "piercing the corporate veil" is a single test.

What is the Law?

As a general rule, there are three situations in which a court will disregard your separate legal entity and decide that your personal assets should be included along with company assets to pay a lawsuit or creditor's claim:

> when the entity is operated as the owner's alter ego;
> when the corporation is under-capitalized; and
> to prevent fraud.

The "alter ego" prong is the most dangerous for domaining companies. In practice, a court is looking for situations in which the owner treats the company bank accounts and records as his own personal bank accounts and records. It is most commonly found when there is only one owner of a company, and where the owner is constantly dipping into company funds to pay personal debts and not keeping good records of these transactions. Essentially, the "alter ego" rule says that if you don't treat your company assets as separate from your own, the courts won't either.

The "under-capitalized" and "prevent fraud" prongs are far less commonly invoked, and thus the requirements meeting those tests are less clear. Generally if you aren't pulling every dollar out of the company as soon as its made so that your company is constantly teetering on the point of failure, then you meet the "under-capitalized" prong. The final prong, "to prevent fraud" is just a general catch-all prong which allows courts to disregard a legal entity when they feel like someone has complied with the letter, but not the spirit, of the law.

How to Stay Out of Trouble?

Never borrow money from the company for personal expenses if you can avoid it. If you have to do it, make sure that you keep very accurate records of how much was borrowed, and when it was paid back. To be safe you should also charge yourself a reasonable interest rate for the money borrowed.

Always keep separate financial records for your personal accounts and your business. When purchasing or selling a domain make sure to do so in the company's name, not in your own, so there is never any doubt who is transacting.

Consider that even if you keep meticulous records and otherwise treat your company as a separate entity from yourself, the "prevent fraud" catch-all test will always provide wiggle room for a court to disregard your separate legal status. So you may want to consider not owning 100% of your company, as companies with divided ownership interests are almost never legally disregarded by courts.

Tax Treatment of Domains

Is your business a "business" or just a "hobby"?

Starting a domaining company involves some initial cash outlays to buy your first round of domains, but often the revenue doesn't come until much later. Therefore, domaining companies commonly lose money their first few years. Just because a company loses money, doesn't mean it's not a legitimate company; after all, most of the airline companies lose money in their initial years of operation. But for the IRS, showing losses in more than two out of any five years is an automatic trigger that your business will be treated as a "hobby" for tax purposes.

What is the Law?
For domaining companies in particular, it is important to be treated as a "business" and not a "hobby" because you cannot deduct the losses from a "hobby." That means that you will not be able to use the losses in the early years of your company to offset the profits you make as the company matures, ultimately subjecting your company to paying much more in taxes.

The IRS has made the "more than two out of any five" rule because they want to discourage people from creating fake companies just to get tax deductions. Without the rule, for example, someone might start a "food review" company which never turns a profit, but through which the person can deduct all of their meals as business expenses. But since there are obviously a lot of legitimate companies that lose money in more than two out of any five years, there is a set of alternative indicators which a company can use to show that it is in fact a "business" and not a "hobby." The alternative factors are as follows:

- You carry on the activity in a businesslike manner.
- The time and effort you put into the activity indicate you intend to make it profitable.
- You depend on income from the activity for your livelihood.
- Your losses are due to circumstances beyond your control (or are normal in the start-up phase of your type of business).
- You change your methods of operation in an attempt to improve profitability.
- You, or your advisors, have the knowledge needed to carry on the activity as a successful business.

You were successful in making a profit in similar activities in the past.

The activity makes a profit in some years.

You can expect to make a future profit from the appreciation of the assets used in the activity.

How to Stay Out of Trouble?

Never make any formal representation that your company is "just a hobby." Your company is a for-profit company, and your financial records should indicate your intent to reach profitability.

Always include in your annual financial records an indication that you are aware of your company's lack of profits and detail your plans for achieving profitability. Whether your plan is as simple as waiting until your domains have appreciated enough to sell them, or as complex as changing your business structure, it is important to have a plan to profitability in writing if your company is losing money.

Consider that accountants are largely unfamiliar with domaining companies, thus, they might simply view the business as a hobby or some illegitimate tax-evasion scheme. As a consequence, it is important that you insist on treating your company as a "business" and not a "hobby" for tax purposes, and to explain the reasons why to your accountant.

Donating Domain Names

Domaining is still an illiquid market. Although everyone agrees that www.CreditCards.com is worth a lot more than www.buy-your-credit-card-here.com, the actual value of either site might vary from estimates by more than 100% based upon whether the right buyer comes along. Faced with the proposition of selling what in the right buyer's hands is a $100,000 domain for a mere $10,000, a lot of domainers decide that they'd rather donate the domain name to their favorite charity and take the full value of the site ($100,000) as a tax deduction. Unfortunately, however, the law on how much you can deduct for your domain donations is less friendly than most domainers would suspect.

What is the Law?
The real issue is how you classify your domains for tax purposes. They could be intellectual property, inventory, business assets, government licenses, a form of real estate, or a host of other things. The truth is, nobody really knows yet how they should be treated, so together accountants and domainers are taking their best guess and hoping they don't get audited. At this point that's about all you have to go on, so the best thing you can do is be aware of your options.

If you decide to treat your domains as intellectual property, analogizing a domain to a trademark, you can only deduct the lesser of your cost basis in the domain or the fair market value. Assuming the domain name has increased in value since you bought it, that means that you only get to deduct the amount you paid for the domain minus any depreciations you have made.

Treating your domains as inventory is similarly limited to the lesser of your cost basis or the fair market value. Again, assuming the domain has increased in value during the time you've held it, that means you only get to deduct the amount you paid for it, which may make donating the domain no longer worth it.

The only categorization of domains that really helps you when it comes to making donations, is treating your domains as long-term business assets. Domains which are classified as long-term business assets and which your company has held for over one year can be deducted at the full fair market value.

How to Stay Out of Trouble?
Never take a sizeable deduction without some documentation. If you're doing your own taxes, the best way to stay clear of really big problems is to document everything. Get a third party appraiser before a donation, and if you don't want to do that, at least have a listing of the selling prices of comparable domains during that timeframe so you can show some support for your deduction. Also consider that if the charity sells the domain, you can use the actual selling price as the fair market value for determining the deduction.

Always stay consistent in the way you you decide to categorize your domains. A surefire way to get nailed in an audit is to treat your domains as business assets in one area and inventory in another. Whatever you pick, stick with it.

Consider that if instead of donating the domain you just don't renew it, the IRS will let you deduct as a loss the amount you paid for the domain above the registration cost (minus any depreciation you've already taken).

Depreciating v. Deducting Your Domains

Let's say in year one of your domaining business you make $1,000 and you spend $1,000 in purchasing new domains ... no income tax right? Probably not. One of the most controversial issues with running a domaining business is how to deduct and / or depreciate your domains. If you aren't familiar with tax law, deducting a business expense means that you get to subtract 100% of that cost from your revenue to calculate your income. Depreciation, by contrast, means that you only get to subtract part of the cost of the business expense in year 1, and another percentage in year 2, and so on. The bottom line is that you generally want deductions rather than depreciations because it means you pay less in taxes now.

The IRS has categories of goods, some of which qualify for deduction and others for depreciation, unfortunately, there is no clear category for domains, so that leaves domainers and their accountants guessing.

What is the Law?
Although many domainers deduct in full their domain purchases, most tax experts agree that they should be depreciated in some way. Where they disagree is over how many years they need to be depreciated. IRS Publication 946 lays out the various categories, and include 7-years as the default for any property that doesn't fit elsewhere. While there are a few tax experts arguing that there should be a depreciation schedule that is longer than 7-years (or none at all), this is probably a reasonably safe position. If you want to get aggressive with your tax deductions, you're probably safe depreciating your domains over 5-years since most general business assets fall into that category, but trying to prove that a domain name has anything shorter than a 5-year shelf life may be hard to pull off if you get audited.

How to Stay Out of Trouble?
Always deduct in full the registration fee for any new registration domains you buy. When you buy a previously unregistered domain, the entire price you pay is the registration fee which is fully

deductible. Again, "deductible" means you get to subtract it 100% from your revenue all in the current year, so this is a big tax advantage over depreciation.

Never depreciate your assets according to a useful life of less than 5 years, unless you've got some really good tax advice and possibly even an opinion letter from an accountant saying he thinks you're on strong ground.

Consider that a lot of the other purchases you make also have to be depreciated (not deducted). For example, your work computer gets depreciated over 5 years, while office furniture and equipment gets depreciated over 7 years.

Five Summarizing Tips for Domainers

We've covered quite a bit in this chapter, but it all boils down to one thing... be careful with your investments!

1. Instead of registering brand names, product names, or slogans you should choose generic dictionary words and imaginative terms that you dreamed up.

2. Always use accurate contact information.

3. Don't register domain names with the intent to sell them to a trademark holder.

4. Never forward your traffic to competing websites and always monitor your parking ads to ensure you don't step on anybody's toes – especially if your domain is

"confusingly similar" to a trademark.

5. Respect the law and don't ignore Cease and Desist letters.

By choosing the right domains and conducting business in an honest manner, you'll have a much better chance of avoiding the major legal issues within domaining.

Chapter 14 - General Economic Trends

In This Chapter...

> ✓ **Domain Growth (long-term increase in value)**
> ✓ **The Future of Business**

Domain Growth

People often compare domaining to the gold rush. At one point in time there were thousands upon thousands of high-end domains available for registration fee, but then the floodgates opened and it was much more difficult to strike it rich.

During the California Gold Rush of 1849, about 20% of the gold-seekers made a modest profit while the rest, especially those arriving late, made little or even ended up losing money. While you might think you're late to the recent domain rush, you're not! Things are just starting to heat up.

It's true that years ago people merely had to spend a few thousand (or less) on domains that would later be worth millions – such as Rick Schwartz who bought Men.com for $15,000 in 1997 and sold it for $1.3 million less than seven years later. But just because you won't find deals like that doesn't mean there isn't a fortune to be had.

As more people and businesses move online, the industry will continue to move forward. Much like real estate in a busy city, there is a limit to the number of high end properties available. As demand for these domain names grows, so will the value.

The number of registrations will continue to rise as more people turn to the internet for news, social networking, business, shopping, leisure, and entertainment.

Today, billions of people in the world don't even have constant access to internet like many of us have grown used to – meaning there is still plenty of room for the industry to expand in the years to come.

Sure it would have been great to get in ten years ago, but there are also benefits to getting in now: rules have been established, systems have been built, and you can learn winning strategies from others that have experienced the good and the bad.

The Future of Business

It has been said that the average person takes a mere 3 seconds to judge a website. In online business, first impressions are a big deal – and what better way is there for businesses to make an impression than to have a great domain name with relevant keywords?

As companies continue to realize the growing potential of online marketing, the value of domains will be on the rise. And to be blunt – there's no way this will *not* happen.

Businesses have already spent billions of dollars on web development, pay-per-click advertising, search engine optimization, article marketing, ad networks, affiliate marketing, opt-in programs, email campaigns, and more.

In the competitive business world, marketers are constantly pushing for new ways to find an edge. While offline advertising is often ineffective and difficult to track, internet marketing has established itself as a reliable, and often better, alternative.

Businesses can analyze detailed information about their visitors – where they came from, how long they stayed on the site, what pages they viewed, and where they went afterwards – and even personalize their ads so they will only be displayed to internet users that fit their ideal demographic profile.

Companies can manage and track their newsletter open ratios, sales page conversion rates, and click-through rates for online ads. If something is performing poorly it is easy to discover and tweak before *voila*, everything is back on track.

Simply stated – the internet is the place to be for business owners.

If you think the domaining gold rush has come and gone then you're missing out on the thousands of nuggets surrounding you *right now*.

Too many domainers wonder what it would have been like if they entered the industry ten years ago. You can't change the past, but you can build your future. Ten years from today you'll be patting yourself on the back for investing in domains.

Chapter 15 - Conclusion

In This Chapter...

- ✓ Ready, Set, GO!
- ✓ The Next Step...

Ready, Set, GO!

Congratulations for making it this far! Most people dream of success, but very few prepare for it. The simple fact that you've completed this book shows you have the right attitude for making money online through domaining.

As you can tell by now, domaining is no simple task...but *anybody* can do it if they understand the key strategies for success that I've outlined for you.

It is true that almost all the good names have been taken and you won't be able to make a million in minutes. But you don't need to make a million right away. This isn't a pipe dream, it's a business. By meticulously building your portfolio you can create an ever growing and never ending stream of revenue!

You know the potential and you understand the key strategies for success. Congrats on coming this far, but now it's time for you to act!

The Next Step…

I've provided a number of resources. I encourage you to find the ones that work best for you and to use them whenever you get down to business.

In the next chapter I have also provided a list of industry blogs and forums. I highly recommend reading these resources as they'll keep you updated with the industry for years to come.

I wish you the best of luck with your future investments and I sincerely hope to see you around the domainersphere for years to come. Kind regards,

Jerome Robertson

Chapter 16 - Further Reading

In This Chapter...

- ✓ Blogs
- ✓ Forums

Further Reading:

No matter how much you know about domaining, there is always more to learn. On top of that, you'll need to keep on top of trends in the domaining world. The best way to do both of these is reading domain blogs and joining domain forums.

The number one source - a must read if you only have time for one - is DNJournal. Every week Ron Jackson reports the top sales of the previous week, which are worth poring over to get a good idea as to what kind of domains are selling and for what prices. As well, Ron regularly writes feature articles profiling a domainer or domain company in detail.

One of the easiest ways to keep up with all the blogs is through a domain aggregator. There are three main aggregators – Namebee, and Domaining.

Leading Blogs:

CircleID: A complete social media hub for the internet's infrastructure and policies.
Domain Name Wire: Andrew Allemann and other industry experts fill you in on the latest news.
DomainGang: - A satirical blog which is often closer to the truth than the news blogs.
DomainShane: Part-time domainer offers a refreshing approach to blogging.
Domain Sherpa: Website provides in-depth video interviews about the industry.
DomainInvesting: Elliot Silver maintains one of the top blogs in the domain industry – a "must read".
Morgan Linton: Morgan shares a lot of his practical experience in the industry.
The Domains: Regular news and updates from around the industry.
TLD Investors: Run by one of the domain industry's best bloggers.
Whizzbang's Blog: Loads of insightful news and domain news commentary.

Domain Forums:

Domain forums are a great way to learn more about the industry, make contacts and friends, and buy and sell domain names to other domainers.

There are two main generalist domain forums: **DNForum and NamePros**. Both are worth joining. Each has their own personality. NamePros caters more to beginners whereas DNForum, while it welcomes beginners, tends to have a crowd that has been in the business for longer. DNForum is free to join, but it costs money to sell your domains there.

[DomainBoardroom](#) is a private domain forum at which you need to be approved to join.

A number of webmaster forums have domain sections. These often aren't worth focusing a lot of time on but if you are into developing domains they can be helpful. The main webmaster forums with domain sections are [DigitalPoint](#), [v7n](#), [WebmasterWorld](#), and [WebHostingTalk](#).

If you are interested in cctlds, there is a domaining forum for pretty much every cctld that is popular with investors:
.co.uk - [AcornDomains](#)
.de - [ConsultDomain](#), and [DomainForum](#)
.ca - [DomainNamesCanada](#)
.in - [INForum](#)
.com.au - [DNTrade](#)
.pl - [Domeny Internetowe](#)
.ru - [DomenForum](#)
.es - [ForoDominios](#)
IDNs - [IDNForums](#)

The cctld and niche domaining forums tend to be smaller and quieter. This means that there is a much higher signal to noise ratio in these forums as well as a much greater sense of camaraderie.

Overwhelmed by the large choice of forums? I recommend starting at either DNForum or NamePros, and then branching out form there.

Once you get into things more seriously, consider attending a domain conference. The most popular one and the best for beginners is [NamesCon](#).

Disclaimer

The information in this document is intended for the sole purpose of education. While I have done everything possible to provide accurate information that is both up-to-date and reliable, no warranties or guarantees of any kind are expressed or implied.

The reader must acknowledge that the author is not engaged in rendering legal, financial, or professional advice and in absolutely no circumstance is either Jerome Robertson responsible for any losses incurred as a direct or indirect result of information within this document, including but not limited to errors, omissions, or inaccuracies.

Copyright Notice

Copyright 2016 by Jerome Robertson

This document is intended for personal use only. No part of this document may be sold, distributed, edited, or modified in any way without the express written consent of Jerome Robertson.

www.ingramcontent.com/pod-product-compliance
Lightning Source LLC
Chambersburg PA
CBHW071432180526
45170CB00001B/314